ALBANIA

Corfu

GREECE

The
Ionian
Islands

Lefkas

Ithaki

Kefalonia

N
W E *MEDITERRANEAN*
S *SEA*

0   40miles
0   60Km

Zakynthos

MEDITERRANEAN SUNSEEKERS
KEFALONIA

Brian & Eileen Anderson

MPC

Contents

Introduction	7
Greek National Tourist Office	8
A Touch of Geography	9
A Little Geology	9
When To Go	12
Climate	13
Where To Go	13
Getting There	17
Passports and Jabs	17
Essential Things to Pack	20
Food and Drink	20
The People	25
Arts and Culture	29
Flora and Fauna	29
Holiday Reading	32
A Little Light History	32
The Mycenaeans	32
Emergence of City States	32
The Roman Period	33
The Byzantine Period (AD337-1267)	33
The Orsini Family (1194-1357)	36
The Tocco Dynasty (1357-1479)	36
Venetian Rule	37
French and Russian Masters (1797-1809)	40
The British Rule (1809-1864)	40
Union with Greece	41
Out and About	**42**
Good Beach Guide	44
A Day Out in Argostoli	45
A Day in Fiskardo	53
A Day in Lixouri	57
A Trip to Ithaka	61
Car Tours	
1: The Northern Peninsula Angonas/Myrtos Beach/ Assos/ Emblisi Beach/ Fiskardo	72
2: Caves and Crags Agrapidiaes Pass/Drogarati Cave/Sami/Anti Samos/ Melissani Cave/Ag Efimia	76
3: Saints George and Gerassimos Agrapidiaes Pass/Ag Gerassimos/Robola Producers Co-operative/ Markopoulo/Tzanata/Mount Atros/Skala/Kato Katelios Lourdas Beach	84

4 Southern Resorts   88

Excursions from the Island	
Olympia	
The Palaistra/The Temple of Hera/The Temple of Zeus/ Nymphaion Fountain/ Treasuries/The Stadium/ Archaeological Museum	93
Athens	97
Tour 1: Ancient Athens: The Acropolis and the Agora The Sacred Way/The Beule Gate/The Propylaia/ The Temple of Athena Nike/ The Erechtheion/The Acropolis Museum/The Parthenon/The Theatre of Dionysos/The Asklepion/ The Stoa of Eumenes/ Odeon of Herod Atticus/ The Peripatos/The Areopagus (Hill of Ares)/ The Agora	97
Tour 2: Hill of the Muses: Filopappou Hill and The Pnyx Fillopappou Hill/Pnyx Hill/ Hill of the Nymphs	104
Tour 3: Panorama: Kolonaki Square/Dexameni Square	

Likavitos Hill	105
Tour 4: The National Archaeological Museum	105
Tour 5: Old Athens: Plaka/ Tower of the Winds/Flea Market	108
Tour 6: Shopping	109
Facts for Visitors	**110**
Accommodation	110
Hotels	110
Villas and Apartments	110
Camping	112
Car Hire	112
Motorcycles	113
Changing Money	113
Consulates	113
Crime and Theft	116
Currency and Credit Cards	116
Driving on Kefalonia	117
Road Signs	120
Accidents and Legal Advice	120
Breakdowns	120
Disabled Facilities	120
Electricity	121
Emergency Telephone Numbers	121
Greek Time	121
Health Care	121
Health Hazards	124
Holiday Insurance	124
International Dialling Codes	124
Language	125
The Alphabet	125
Numbers	125
Days of the Week	128
Useful Phrases	128
Place Names	129
Lost Property	129
Maps	129
Mosquitoes	132
Museums	132
National Tourist Office	132
Newspapers and Magazines	132
Nightlife	132
Nudism	132

Pets	132
Pharmacies	133
Photography	133
Postal Services	133
Public Holidays and Festivals	133
Cultural Events	136
Public Toilets	136
Public Transport	136
Buses	136
Taxis	137
Shopping	137
Sports and Pastimes	137
Windsurfing	137
Water-skiing and Jet Skiing	137
Scuba diving	137
Tennis	137
Horse riding	137
Walking	139
Sailing	139
Sunbathing	139
Swimming	140
Telephone Services	140
Tipping	140
Water	140

Maps	
Ionian Islands	1
Kefalonia	22/23
Argostoli	50

Feature Boxes	
Sunseeker Hot Spots	10/11
Sunseeker Hot Spots	14/15
Mainland Hopping	18
Fast Food Greek Style	26
The Kefalonia Fir	30
Sunseeker Tips	46/47
The Earthquake of 1953	51
Eating Out in Argostoli	54
The Monk Seal	58
Odysseus on Ithaka and Kefalonia	66
The Wines of Kefalonia	86
Consular Help	114
Clothes Sizes	138

Index	**141**

KEY TO SYMBOLS USED IN TEXT MARGIN AND ON MAPS

🚶 Recommended walks

🐟 Aquatic interest

🏰 Castle/Fortification

✳ Other place of interest

🤿 Beach

⛵ Water sports

🌸 Garden

⛪ Church/Ecclesiastical site

🏢 Building of interest

🏛 Archaeological site

🖼 Museum/Art Gallery

🌄 Beautiful view/Scenery, Natural phenomenon

🐦 Birdlife

✈ Airport

🐎 Nature Reserve/Animal interest

🚩 Golf

🚂 interesting Railway

🦇 Caves

🍀 Parkland

⛰ Mountain/Notch

ℹ Tourist information

KEY TO MAPS

——————— Main Routes (Surfaced)

——————— Secondary Routes (Surfaced)

----------- Track

Town

River/Lake

HOW TO USE THIS GUIDE

Enjoying as much sun and fun on a vacation is everyone's dream. *Mediterranean Sunseekers: Kefalonia* will help to make this dream come true. Your guide has been designed in easy to use sections.

'The Introduction is packed with detailed information on the island, its history, geography, people, culture, food and much more. 'Out and About Kefalonia' is a comprehensive itinerary covering the island with a series of useful and practical motoring or walking tours. Many places are off the beaten track and not on the usual tourist circuit. 'Facts for Visitors' arranged in alphabetical order for easy reference, lists practical information and useful advice to help you plan your vacation before you go and while you are there.

Distinctive margin symbols in the text and on maps, plus places to visit highlighted in bold enable the reader to find the most interesting places with ease.

Introduction

A rugged island of sharp land-scapes, countless bays and inlets and fine beaches, Kefalonia has been hiding its light under a bushel for years. Only recently have the island's farmers and fishermen looked towards tourism as a new industry and how quickly the island is succeeding.

No Greek island is quite the same as another no matter how physically close they may lie and Kefalonia is a new and different experience which has already gathered a following of devotees intent on returning year after year. Scenery makes the first impression, it is so different to its Ionian neighbours. Not here the luscious green mantle of Corfu or the pastoral ambience of Zakinthos (Zante), instead stark, grey limestone mountains thrust high to meet an achingly blue sky. More scenic touches are added by the highly indented coastline with headlands, bays, peninsulas, inlets within inlets and beaches of great natural beauty as at Myrtos.

If the scenery provides the backdrop, people and culture provide the interest. The tradition of friendliness found throughout the Ionian Islands is found in good measure on Kefalonia. Do not expect to see an old way of life on the island. Kefalonia's cultural heritage may well stretch back to Mycenaean times, and there are rich traces still to be seen around the island, but the thread of history is not continu-ous. A massive earthquake in 1953 proved to be one of those staggering events which totally reset the course of the island. It emerged from total devastation to rebuild from the ruins but old ways, old habits and old customs disappeared with the earthquake only to be reborn in modern ways in new surroundings.

Now the island looks to tourism and its resorts are in the development phase. There is no headlong rush, the path into tourism is being taken quite slowly and it is wrong to think of the island as one great builders yard. Most of the resorts are comparatively small but all the services are in place to help the visitor make the most of the day but not necessarily of the night. It is a place to relax, to enjoy the beach, catch some sightseeing, delve into Mycenaean history, eat well and feel content.

Kefalonia is really two islands for the price of one. Just a short sail away is Ithaka, another island awaiting exploration. Homeric associations lie around every corner and it is a place to let fantasies run freely while exploring its harbours and villages.

GREEK NATIONAL TOURIST OFFICE

Leaflets on Kefalonia, the Ionian Islands and general information on Greece is available before depar-

Preceding Page: The harbour at Assos

ture from the Greek National Tourist Office, addresses as follows:

UK and Ireland, 4 Conduit Street, London W1R 0DJ ☎ 0171 734 599

USA, 645 Fifth Avenue, Olympic Tower (5th Floor), New York NY10022 ☎ 421 57777;

168 North Michigan Avenue, Chicago, Illinois 60601 ☎ 728 1084

611 West 6th Street, Suite 2198 Los Angeles, California 90017 ☎ 626 696

Australia and New Zealand, 51-57 Pitt Street, Sydney, NSW 2000 ☎ 241 1663

A Touch of Geography

Kefalonia, with an area of 688sq km, is the largest of the seven Ionian Islands but with around only 32,000 inhabitants is not the most populous. Lying almost opposite the entrance to the Gulf of Patras, it is located between Lefkas to the north and Zante to the south. Mountains dominate the island with the highest peak, Mt Ainos, in the south reaching an altitude of 1,626m (5,335ft) but there are as many as ten peaks topping 900m (2,953ft). Extending out to the west is the extensive Lixouri (Paliki) peninsula which encloses the Gulf of

Argostoli. This is less mountainous than the rest of the island and is best described as hilly. Its irregular shape makes quoting dimensions difficult but on a north to south axis it is around 32km (20miles) long and east to west 27km (17 miles) but that also includes the Gulf of Argostoli. All the major settlements are located around the coast with only smaller villages tucked away in the hills.

Livathos plain, just south of Argostoli is one of the largest and most fertile of the island's plains which are few and small. Collectively these plains are sufficient to sustain an important agricultural sector producing olives, grapes, figs withother fruit and vegetables. Livestock also contributes to the econ-omy and the mountains are used to sustain large herds of goats. Fishing is the other mainstay of the economy with tourism, a new growth industry, starting to make an impact.

A Little Geology

Kefalonia consists largely of limestone rock formations in permeable stratas which are not dissimilar to the karst formations seen along the Adriatic coast. Slowly but steadily over aeons of time, rainwater acidified by the carbon dioxide of the atmosphere permeates and dissolves these limestones to generate caverns, caves and swallow holes. Caves the island certainly has and two of these,

Sunseeker
Hot Spots

Places not to be missed on Kefalonia:

Above: Argostoli. Good waterside atmosphere, delightful main square, pedestrianised shopping, excellent fruit market and museums

Below: Assos. Scenic position on the neck of a peninsula, natural beauty, intimate atmosphere and Venetian castle

Above: Fiskardo. Delightful yachting harbour, atmospheric water front, ancient remains

Below: Melissani Cave. Watery cave explored by boat

Dragomati and Melissani caves have become tourist features but equally fascinating is the island's swallow holes.

The entrance to the swallow holes lie just north of Argostoli, towards the tip of the peninsula. Sea water disappears down the hole with such force that, in the nineteenth century, an Englishman built a water mill to harness the energy. It was only in 1963 that a team of Austrian geologists, with the aid of 160kg of a soluble red dye, were fully able to determine with certainty the path taken by the water. The flow is easterly beneath the island collecting rainwater percolating through the mountain mass en route. Some of the flow emerges into the lake in Melissani cave whilst the rest discharges into the sea off the coast of Sami.

WHEN TO GO

Easter time in April is about the earliest that can be considered. Even at this time there is a risk that the weather will be cold and showery but, if the sun is shining, the island is at its most beautiful. At this time the sea is still cold but the sun is easily hot enough to burn and sunbathers still need to take care. Spring is a delightful season for colour when the trees are vivid green and the wild flowers at their very best. Fortunately, the spring flowers extend into May and this month is generally more reliable for weather. Daytime tempera-tures start to rise but the evenings are still cool. It is not always warm enough to dine outside in the evening in the early part of the month but night-time tempera-tures too are on the rise and it soon becomes possible, well before the month is out. The island has plenty of visitors in these early months but not enough to make it busy with the result that, although bars and tavernas are usually in full swing, some of the water sports have not yet opened.

Things warm up in June in every sense. The days and nights get hotter and the island tourist machine moves into top gear. Nowhere is too crowded and independent visitors can still expect to find accommodation without too much trouble, except in the Lassi area which is fully booked to tour operators. All that changes in July, with the Greeks and Italians moving into their holiday season, and the island suddenly becomes very crowded. July and August are the hottest months of the year and the least comfortable on the island. Beaches are full and the facilities often at full stretch.

Even the locals welcome September when the crowds have departed and some of the intense heat leaves the sun. Many regard September as the best month of the summer with the sea still warm and the sun still pouring incessantly from the sky although the autumn rains may well start before the month is out. October is cooler with more cloudy and rainy days but still with fine, sunny periods.

CLIMATE

Kefalonia enjoys a fairly typical Mediterranean climate which in simple terms means mild, wet winters and hot dry summers. Overall, Kefalonia has a high annual rainfall, somewhere in the region of 42.5in (108cm), which is similar to Corfu but higher than most other Greek islands and almost three times more than Crete. Fortunately for holidaymakers, most of this rain falls in the winter months, between October and March. Summers are not entirely without rain but usually in the form of thunderstorms which may be heavy but short lived. All this translates to good news for summer visitors, the heavy winter rainfall ensures the vegetation stays green throughout the whole year and that taps do not run dry or showers dry up at the height of the tourist season.

January and February are the coldest months and even then average maximum daytime temperatures of around 14°C are enjoyed. Although a sprinkling of snow on Mt Ainos is frequently seen, frost at sea level is rare. Spring comes early, judging by the flowers, as early as February but March and April are the main spring months. Sometimes the increase in temperatures from spring to summer is steady but just occasionally it is very rapid and the summer heat starts early.

Summer is long and hot with May and June averaging daily more than 10 and 11 hours of sunshine respectively while July and August enjoy around 12 and 13.

Autumn rains arrive fairly early in Kefalonia compared to other Greek islands, usually sometime in September although temperatures stay fairly high. October starts the six really wet months of winter but even then more than 6 hours of sunshine are still expected every day.

Kefalonia is cooled in summer by the maestro blowing from the north west which can rise in the afternoon only to settle again in the evenings. Although not too frequent, the worst of the winds is the sirocco blowing up from North Africa which brings a heavy haze and hot, sticky conditions.

WHERE TO GO

Resort Guide
Holiday brochures try to make each and every resort sound attractive without always revealing too much about its character. This guide offers a quick outline of the main resorts on the island to help in making the most suitable choice. A more detailed description of the resorts may be found by consulting the Out and About section and those marked with an asterisk are also featured in the Good Beach Guide which is included in the next section. Water sport facilities are indicated by symbols. One ⬧ indicates very limited facilities, per-

Sunseeker
Hot Spots

Places not to be missed on Kefalonia:

Above: Lassi and Gialos Beaches. Fine sandy beaches, water sports and tourist facilities

Below: Myrtos Beach. Scenic beach of white sand

Above: Ithaka (Ithaki). Mountainous island, pretty fishing villages and attractive main town.

Below: Dragorati Cave. Cave to explore on foot

haps just pedaloes or simply boats for hire, while the maximum three indicates the whole gamut from paragliding, jet skis, banana rides down to the less energetic pursuits but remember, full facilities are not always available early and late in the season. Night life has barely developed on the island and even the disco in Argostoli only opens at weekend.

Starting from Argostoli, the resorts are presented in clockwise direction around the island.

Argostoli: as the capital town it seems dedicated to pleasure and relaxation. It may not have a resort atmosphere but it has a lot in its favour; an interesting waterfront, probably the best eating on the island, some nightlife and it is the hub of the bus network. The main square is the place to see and be seen in the evening. There is no immediate beach but Lassi with its beaches is but a short taxi ride away.

Lassi*: lying fairly close to Argostoli, this is perhaps the major resort area on the island. It has a number of fine, sandy beaches which are its biggest asset but, as a resort, it lacks character. Much of the development, shops, restaurants and accommodation, straggle along the busy main road leading to the airport. ⛵ ⛵ ⛵

Svoronata: small resort almost adjacent to the airport although Kefalonia is not the busiest airport in Greece. Consists largely of accommodation and a small sandy beach.

Lourdas Beach*: unspoilt resort with a long stretch of sandy beach. Rather isolated with the nearest village, Lourdata considerably uphill and the main road still higher.

Kato Katelios: a small, sleepy resort in the south of the island developing around a fishing harbour. Good atmosphere with tavernas on hand, expect far more sand than people. ⛵

Skala*: Scenically situated at the foot of the mountains, the village centres on a pine clad headland. large enough to have some life with a good selection of tavernas, cafés and shops along the main street. Good beach of mainly sand. Isolated from the point of view of visiting other places on the island. ⛵ ⛵

Poros: although not large by any means, Poros is one of the bigger resorts on the island with an attractive and compact centre. Handy for the ferry to Killini and Lefkas. The beach is narrow and mainly shingle. Like Skala above, it is remote for touring the island. ⛵ ⛵ ⛵

Sami: developed around a natural harbour, waterfront Sami has a surprisingly modern air. It is fairly quiet in the day as visitors walk out either to the shingle beach to the north or make the trek (3km/2 miles) over the hill to the beautiful Anti Samos beach*. ⚓

Fiskardo: picturesque fishing village and yachting centre on the northern tip of the island. Great ambience, very quiet with a small, shingle beach close by. ⚓

Assos: natural beauty spot on the neck of a peninsula. Only a small village with good, relaxing atmosphere; nearest beach is Myrtos.

Lixouri: located on the Paliki Peninsula almost opposite Argostoli. This is the second largest town on the island and dedicated more to work than pleasure but with a good Greek atmosphere. Ferries run non-stop between here and Argostoli. There is no beach immediately on hand but Lepeda beach* is a 30 minute walk or a brief taxi ride to the south.

GETTING THERE

The easiest way is by charter flight directly from a regional airport in the UK and there are a fair number of tour operators offering packaged holidays to the island including Inspirations and Thomsons. Travel agents generally only deal with a limited number of tour operators and if they are unable to offer the required destination, they will, on request, find out from a directory which operators do serve the particular resort. It may be necessary to change to a travel agent who deals with the company to book a holiday.

For those planning to stay longer than the usual two or three weeks, it may be necessary to travel on scheduled flights from London to Athens then from Athens to Kefalonia. There are many carriers offering flights to Athens but only Olympic Airways flying between Athens and Kefalonia. This may change shortly since there are now a number of new carriers in Greece opening up flights to the islands. Usually the journey from the UK can be accomplished in one day without the need for an overnight stop in Athens.

The scheduled route into Athens with an onward flight to Kefalonia is the only option from North America, although many Americans find it more economical to fly into London and join a packaged holiday. Flights from America to Athens may not connect up conveniently with the limited Kefalonia flights. If an overnight stop is required there is a hotel reservations desk at Athens airport. Hotels near the airport tend to be noisy so, for a quieter night, it is better to choose a city centre hotel.

PASSPORTS AND JABS

There are no visa requirements for EU citizens or other English speaking nationals (USA, Australia, Canada, New Zealand) for visits of up to 3 months. All that is required is a valid passport.

Mainland Hopping

Kefalonia makes a very convenient base for a two centre holiday but it needs a little planning beforehand. With a hire car it is very easy to escape by ferry from Poros over to Killini in the Peloponnese which instantly opens up a whole new range of possibilities. Here are a few suggestions:

A southern route could incorporate Olympia, easily reached within the first day, (see page 93 for more details) and then on to explore the Mani, the southern central peninsula of the Peloponnese. Mani, a wild and rugged refuge for fugitives in the past, is friendly enough now but the hints of hostility in the castle-like tower houses and the terrain makes this a place apart in Greece. The ruins of medieval Mistra are not that far away and could be incorporated into the return journey.

Using a northern route, Corinth and the Argolid could be a target destination. En route there is a great little rack-and -pinion railway to try out, from Diakopto on the coast to the mountain village of Kalavrita. The Argolid, stronghold of the Mycenaeans, has an abundance of ancient sites to explore including Mycenae itself and Ancient Corinth. Nafplio or nearby Tolon are ideal bases for exploring this region.

A trip to Delphi is easily accomplished within the day although a one or two night stop is recommended to leave time to absorb and enjoy the site of the ancient oracle. The route from Killini is to head north and ferry over from Rio to Andirio on the northern mainland. From Andirio it is basically a coastal run east to Itea then a short leg inland to Delphi.

Details of all these locations can be found in Visitor's Guide to Greece (Moorland Publishing Co. Ltd).

Two neighbouring Ionian islands, Lefkas and Zakinthos (Zante), are within easy reach of Kefalonia. Fiskardo and Sami have daily ferry services to Lefkas. Fiskardo ferries serve both Vasiliki, in the south, and Nidri on the east coast while Sami ferries call in at Ithaka on the way.

For Zakynthos (Zante), ferries leave from Pessada, reached via Peratata, and dock at Ag Nikolaos at the northern tip of the island.

For further details of Zakynthos see the Sunseekers guide.

Above: Olympia is a popular day excursion from Kefalonia

Below: Try the freshly caught fish in one of Argostoli's excellent tavernas

Certain inoculations are advisable for all travellers (hepatitis A, tetanus, typhoid and TB) but none are mandatory for Greece.

ESSENTIAL THINGS TO PACK

Since Greece is a full member of the EU, it is very likely that, should you forget your favourite brand of toothpaste, you will be able to buy it in the shops there. All leading brands of food and products are freely available, give or take some national peculiarities. Brands of tea and breakfast cereal fall into this category, however, a limited range of breakfast cereals can be bought in most tourist regions. With tea it is a little easier, if you have a favourite brand of tea or tea bags then it is easy to find room for some in your luggage.

There are a few other items which are worth considering if only to save time shopping when you are there.

An electric mosquito repeller and tablets — these are readily available in Greece but small travel types are freely available in UK shops which are a convenient size for packing and will last for years. Make sure you buy one with a continental 2 pin plug.

Insect repellent — if you prefer a particular brand, buy it at home.

Anthisan cream for insect bites

Folding umbrella. Particularly if you are visiting Kefalonia outside the main season. Rain showers tend to be short and, with the rain falling straight down, an umbrella gives good protection, better than a waterproof which can quickly make you hot and sweaty.

A small rucksack is useful too for general use when heading for the beach or off on a shopping trip.

Only in early or late season is it necessary to take a heavy jumper but it is always useful to take some thinner layers of clothing which you can wear together if necessary. Sometimes it is cool in the evening or you may feel cool after the heat of the sun. If you intend to do any serious walking make sure you have suitable footwear.

Most basic medical requirements, plasters, bandages, headache pills can be bought in chemist shops on Kefalonia. More than that, many drugs normally available in Britain only on prescription can be bought over the counter on demand and at reasonable prices.

Note that codeine and drugs containing codeine are strictly banned in Greece so be sure to exclude these from your luggage.

FOOD AND DRINK

Watching the Greeks eat is a pleasure in itself. Seldom do they order individually, instead they order a vast number of communal dishes which fill the table to overflowing. They are far less concerned about cold food and many dishes which arrive hot are cold before they are eaten. Some tourists find it a bit disconcerting when their meals are actually served on the cool side but, in most areas, the message that tourists generally like their food hot has registered.

Although the Greek cuisine is quite extensive, tavernas tend only to have a limited menu. Lunch time, between 2 and 3pm after work finishes, is the only meal of the day for which the chef will prepare a range of cooked dishes. For the evening trade, and the Greeks are notoriously late eaters, the menu offers whatever is left over from lunch, which has often been kept warm for hours, and a range of grills which are cooked to order. Charcoal is generally used for grilling and it is not unusual to see large charcoal grills by the doorway or outside in summer. Although the tavernas are the traditional eating places, Argostoli town has a selection of restaurants which provide a better standard of décor in particular and offer a more international cuisine (see feature page 26).

Tavernas are obliged to have a menu but many still do not. Instead diners will be shown a glass show case exhibiting the range of dishes available or, and this is still very common in the villages, they will be led into the kitchen to see exactly what is cooking. If difficulties are experienced in the final choice then spoons may appear for a tasting session. In an effort to improve standards, there has been a recent government decree instructing that all tables should have a cloth tablecloth. Previously it was usual just to have a plain piece of polythene which was changed for each new client. It served a double purpose because at the end of the meal all scraps from the plates would be tipped into it and the whole lot bundled up and removed. Now the situation has changed. Tables are fitted with a decorative table cloth but this is securely protected by a polythene sheet covered by a paper square and only the latter is laid fresh each time. Should there be a menu on the table then it will probably be in Greek and English but it will only show a partial correspondence with the dishes on offer so it still pays to ask. It is unusual to find the table laid, apart from the oil and vinegar flasks, paper napkins and the inevitable toothpicks, but the cutlery arrives with bread after an order is placed.

There is no special form in a taverna and no conventions to follow. The Greeks often go in for a plate of chips and a beer and make it last half the night. For diners though, it is usual to begin with one or a selection of the starters or mezedes on offer. These include tzatsiki (a yoghurt, cucumber and garlic dip), taramasalata (fish roe mixed with potato, oil and vinegar, the pinker the better), melitzano salata (an aubergine dip with tomato and garlic) and humus, another dip this time from chickpeas. Fresh vegetables are rarely available but two vegetables which turn up as mezedes are gigantes (butter beans cooked in tomato and oil) and peas (arakas). Saganaki,

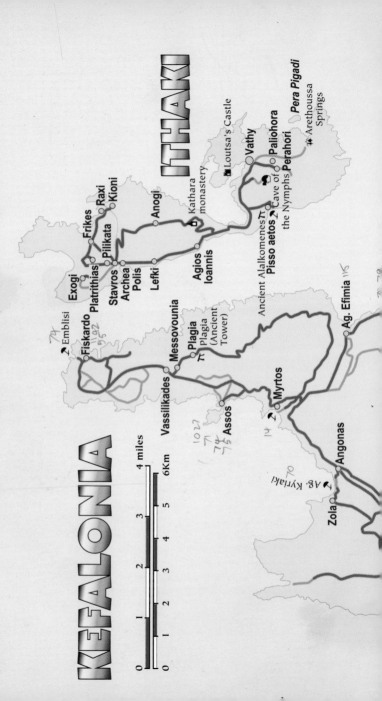

fried cheese, is another interesting starter. The waiter will raise an eyebrow if mezedes are ordered separately by each individual, even tourists are expected to order a selection and share in Greek style. Salads may be preferred as starters or as part of the starters and the most popular is the village salad or horiatiki salata which should include lettuce, or cabbage, but less so now, tomato, onion, cucumber, feta cheese and olives. A few years ago, a salad like this constituted a meal in itself and many tourists were perfectly happy to make a lunch from it. Unfortunately, this made the taverna owner less than happy, consequently the price has risen considerably and they are not always the generous portions they were. Tomatoes, cucumber, feta cheese and lettuce (maruli) are all offered as separate dishes. Ready cooked dishes may include the familiar moussaka, a mince dish with aubergines, potato and bechamel sauce, veal in tomato (kokanista), stifado (veal stew with onions) or giovetsi (oven cooked lamb served with pasta). Chicken cooked on the spit is popular and inexpensive but favoured amongst the grills is souvlaki, veal or pork on a skewer. Chops, pork, lamb or veal, are ever present on the evening menus as are keftedes (spicy meat balls) and biftekia (mince burgers). Kefalonian specialities include sof-rito, veal cooked in wine with herbs, garlic and vinegar and served with a thick sauce and Kefalonian meat pie which has a tasty filling of meat and rice.

Fish is sometimes on offer but for a selection it is better to find a fish taverna, psaria taverna. Fish is becoming increasingly expensive and prices on the menu are often expressed per kilogram which makes them look sky high. In practice, a fish is weighed off and the charge is for that weight. A typical portion is around 400grm. Lobster (astakos) and red mullet (barbounia) are usually top of the menu and are expensive as are shrimps (garides). Octopus, grilled or cooked in wine is less expensive as is squid (kalamari). At the cheap end is the small whitebait (marides) which is eaten in its entirety, head and all. This dish is often available as a starter in a fish restaurant. Desserts are very limited, usually fruit, but the popularity of yoghurt and honey amongst the tourists is now recognised. If you have tucked into your meal with obvious enjoyment, the proprietor may produce a plate of fruit, peeled and presented with his compliments.

Some Greeks prefer to drink ouzo with meals and this is served in small bottles and usually taken with water. Others choose retsina, a resin-ated wine, which is an acquired taste and the popular commercial brand is Kourtaki although Melamatina is equally good and slightly less resin-ated. Most wine lists contain some of the countries acknowledged good wines like Boutari Naoussa and Lac des Roches as well as some medium priced popular ones like Kambas, Rotonda and Domestica. Kefalonia has plenty of vines and a number of wine manufacturers but locals still make their own which is usually good and much cheaper than the branded labels. Ask for 'krasi dopio' (local wine) or 'spitiko krasi' (house wine) which is usually served in a carafe or metal jug.

THE PEOPLE

In spite of the island's turbulent history and a parade of different masters over the centuries, the people of Kefalonia have retained their own brand of Greekness. This Greekness, tempered by western influences, from the Venetians, the French and the British, over the centuries, is a little different from that observed in the more easterly parts but the language and the church provided a continuity which has kept the people in touch with their own identity. Their conviviality and hospitality to strangers wins the island many friends. Sadly, these qualities are subdued by the pressure of work in the height of the tourist season but never squashed. Away from all the bustle, it takes only a cheerful greeting, sometimes only a smile, to be on the receiving end of their hospitality. It may take the form of an orange pulled from a bag or a handful of freshly grown broad beans but whatever it is, it is considered bad manners to refuse. Language barriers do not exist for the Greeks and mostly they will chatter away in their native tongue in the full expect-

ancy that you will understand some or part of whatever they are saying. Body language and gesticulations play a full part too. The head is frequently used this way. Assent is signified by a slight nod to the side and 'no' is indicted by a slight toss of the head upward often accompanied by a slight 'tchh' sound. If words fail, an invitation to come or to follow is mostly by a downward pawing movement of the hand. If this is an invitation into the home, the first offering will be some sweet preserves served with a glass of water. To refuse this is to refuse their hospitality but it is not essential to eat all of it. No matter how poor the hosts, any suggestion of payment will cause deep offence but a small present for a child would be acceptable. The penetration of polite conversation often takes visitors by surprise. After the usual health enquiries, which are taken seriously by the Greeks, the conversation quickly moves into questions about the family, how many sons, daughters and their ages. Unreserved admiration is expressed for parents of large families especially with many sons. From this point enquiries continue about work and will invariably contain a question which throws unprepared visitors almost into a state of shock; 'How much do you earn?' In Greek society in would be considered impolite not to ask.

The family unit is strong and still the basis of Greek society, although there are signs that the bonds are starting to weaken under western influences. It is sons who

Fast Food Greek Style

The Greeks are great nibblers, particularly in the mornings, so there is no shortage of fast-food. Pies with various fillings, usually made with filo pastry and looking like a Cornish pasty:

TIROPITTA: cheese. This is the most universally popular and found everywhere.

SPANAKOPITTA: spinach only or with cheese and eggs. Kreatopitta: minced meat.

PIZZA: usually take-away small ones or sometimes sold as pieces
and for the sweet tooth:

MILOPITTA: apple.

BOUGATZA: vanilla custard.

SOUVLAKI: small pieces of meat on a wooden skewer served with a lump of bread or with pitta.

DONER ME PITTA: slices of meat from the 'gyros' (meat cooked on a vertical spit) placed in a pitta parcel with a little yoghurt, tomato and onion.

TOST: usually a slice of ham and cheese toasted between bread.
Freshly pressed orange juice is widely available.

Above: Poros, which has a shingle beach

Below: Relax in the peace and quiet at Assos

receive the adulation and are totally spoilt by their parents. This does not mean that daughters are not welcomed, as in some societies, and the ideal family is regarded as one son and one daughter. It is remarkable just how many Greek families comprise just two children. In reality they have been using abortion as a means of birth control for a long time. Parental influence is still strong when the time is right for their children to marry. Arranged marriages have not entirely disappeared but they are no longer the norm but parents still have a dominant role in satisfying the demands of society and tradition. It is the duty of the son to stand by his parents to ensure that suitable matches are made for all his sisters before he can contemplate marriage. Although a dowry is no longer a legal requirement, and this repeal was only in recent times, it is still perpetuated. A girl goes into marriage often with the gift of a furnished house or apartment from her parents. It remains the girls property and her security. In the same way gifts of gold to the bride, also to provide for her security, are not unusual. At least the newly wedded couple start life without the burden of debt and are able to build and plan a future for their own children. The family unit extends into business too. The Greek preference is for self employment, failing that a secure job with the state, and most of the small businesses employ only family which are eventually passed down via sons and daughters.

It is a male dominated society in which it is demeaning for a man to indulge in women's tasks. This distinct role division is ingrained into society and a woman would lose face if her man was seen sweeping floors or washing dishes. Attitudes are slowly changing amongst the younger generation. The segregation of the sexes too is inbuilt into society. When family or friends enjoy a meal in a taverna, which can be quite a boisterous affair, there is usually a polarisation where the men cluster to one end of the table and the women to the other. Only men have the freedom to go out alone and it is not uncommon to see them dining out in groups but the young mostly head for the bars and congregate there in large numbers. Again signs of change are evident even in this area and young women are becoming part of the social scene. The role of women in the broader society has been recognised in legislation. They acquired the vote only in 1952 and the first woman Deputy was elected to Parliament the following year. Sexual discrimination in career opportunities and in the place of work has been outlawed. Many practical steps have been taken to assist the integration of women as equals in society. Low cost nurseries providing child places have been provided to free women to work and they have acquired rights of ownership after marriage and an equal share of communal property on divorce. Women now hold important posts in all branches of the Civil Service and in commerce but, in spite of all their progress, equality is only accepted in the big cities. Throughout rural Greece it remains contrary to the culture and fundamental change will only be fully accepted very slowly. For women travelling alone in Greece there are no exceptional problems. The incidence of violent crime, including rape, is much lower than in other western societies. But it is not unknown and the same wariness of the possible situations should be observed. Greek men firmly believe that they are irresistible to all women so their attentions can be expected.

ARTS AND CULTURE

One legacy of the Venetian rule is music which has remained strong on Kefalonia. Argostoli has a well attended Philharmonic School for the teaching of wind and brass instruments and concerts are held from time to time. Lixouri too has a Philharmonic society and most larger towns and villages have their own bands.

Greek dancing is popular on the island and is very often the highlight entertainment at a religious festival. In tourist resorts local dancers often perform in restaurants and tavernas throughout the season. Many of the dances are local to Kefalonia and these show distinct Cretan and Peloponnesian influences arising from historical connections. In addition, programmes usually include the more popular dances performed throughout the country.

FLORA AND FAUNA

Flowers abound in spring from the ubiquitous Spanish broom to rare wild orchids but the best time to see them is from late March through April into May although the season persists longer around the top of Mount Ainos. This latter area is now protected as National Park and one of the species it seeks to protect is the endemic fir tree, *Abies cephalonia*.

Orchids are prominent amongst the spring flora and some 31 different species have been recorded so far and there are probably still more to find.

Despite the heat and the lack of water in summer, there are always a few flowers to be seen, like the beautiful sea daffodil, *Pancratium maritimum*, and the *mulleins*. Autumn rains bring out the crocus and cyclamen in a new flush of flowers which help to keep winter colourful until spring gets into its stride once again.

The fauna is surprisingly good too and the island has a wide range of wild animals including foxes, hares, weasels, pine martens and hedgehogs. The latter is the one most likely to be seen since so many fail to cross the road safely. Wild horses were common on Mt Ainos at one time but no longer. Tortoises are around in great numbers and these

The Kefalonia Fir

Above: Kefalonia fir (*Abies cephalonia*) at Mount Ainos

There was a time when Mount Ainos was heavily forested with *Abies cephalonia*, the Kefalonian fir, which grows above altitudes of around 800m (2,625ft). In mass the trees look very dark which led the Venetians to call this range Monte Nero (the Black Mountain). Forest still exists today but much ravaged by timber demands and repeated fires.

This tree is endemic to the area, not just to the island, and is also found on high ground in much of the southern mainland of Greece. It is a much prized wood and was in demand as soon as man started building wooden ships. The columns at Knossos in Crete were made from Kefalonian fir and it is very possible that the source was this island. Kefalonia had a thriving Mycenaean population at that time which was possibly trading with the Minoans on Crete. Throughout the ages a thriving lumber trade built up largely because Kefalonia's fir forests were accessible and close to the sea for shipping away. In later years the island's forest supplied boatyards in Corfu and Italy.

Forest fires have also played a significant part over the centuries. In 1590 a great part of the forest was lost to fires but over the centuries it regenerated only to suffer an even worse fire in 1797.

In 1962 the area was declared National Park in order to protect this species of fir of which the island is rightly proud.

Above: Paliohora on Ithaka

Below: Ancient Krani showing Mycenaean walls

too are often seen on the road. Greek drivers believe it unlucky to run over a tortoise so they go to great lengths to avoid them.

Snakes are around too in numbers but mostly harmless. Vipers are known to exist but are unlikely to be encountered.

HOLIDAY READING

There is no greater pleasure than reading a book in the location where the book is set, especially when the period is different. Homer's *Odyssey* is by no means heavy going, modern translations of this are in narrative form which read like a novel.

A LITTLE LIGHT HISTORY

The island is particularly rich in pre-historic remains. Significant finds of stone axe-heads, cleavers and ar-row-heads have been made at a number of locations on the island including Sami, Fiskardo and the Argostoli peninsula. Although sci-entific dating is difficult on this type of artefact, they are thought to have arisen around 4,000BC and some scholars put them even earlier. Some of these finds are displayed in the Archaeological museum in Argo-stoli.

The Mycenaeans

Organised civilisation which reach-ed a high degree of sophistication appeared with the Mycenaeans in 1400-1100BC. Kefalonia and neigh-bouring Ithaka were clearly pre-ferred locations for the Mycenaeans since there is nothing comparable on any of the other Ionian islands. Set-tlements were spread around Kef-alonia at Krani, near Argostoli, Pali near Lixouri, Sami and Proni, be-tween Skala and Poros. Since the Mycenaeans built in a robust style with huge blocks of stone, remains of their strongholds have survived pil-fering and earthquakes and are still to be seen at Krani and Sami as well as impressive tombs at Mazarakata. On Ithaka too there was a major set-tlement at Alalkomenes.

Emergence of City States

The Mycenaean period ended around 1100BC when the Dorians invaded from the north wielding superior weapons of iron and Greece entered the Dark Age. Little is known of events on Kefalonia until around the fifth century BC when it appears that some form of democ-racy had emerged paralleling events in mainland Greece. By this time four city states existed based on the old Mycenaean fortified settlements. Each pursued its own policies and there was no united front during the Peloponnesian War (431-404 BC) with support divided between Ath-ens and Corinth. Athens settled the issue by taking the island without resistance and using it as a base of operations. Throughout the fourth century BC there was a greater incli-nation for co-operation between cities throughout the whole of Greece. In this period the Aetolian League formed which eventually all four Kefalonian cities joined. In this period, along with Zakinthos (Zante), they were happily engaged in piracy taking riches from the Achaeans (Peloponnese) and their allies. Around 255BC the Achaeans formed their own league which soon grew into a union of the whole of the Peloponnese. Not too pleased with the constant attentions of the raiders from the Aetolian League, the Achaeans called on King Philip V of Macedonia for assistance. Recognising the strategic importance of Kefalonia, he mounted his first attack against Proni in 218BC but switched to Pali, the most important city on the island at that time. Despite various strategies and attempts, the Macedonians failed.

Meanwhile, Rome and Carthage were at war again in the Second Punic War which lasted from 218 - 202BC in which Philip V of Macedonia allied himself with the Carthaginian general Hannibal. Rome emerged victorious and when asked for help by the eastern Mediterranean Greeks against Philip they readily agreed and easily defeated him. The Roman colonisation of Greece had started.

The Roman Period

Around 189BC, the Romans arrived to take control of Kefalonia and while the other cities capitulated, Sami decided on closing its gates and defending against the ag-gressor. After a siege lasting four months Sami was forced to surrender and the Romans promptly turned Kefalonia into a naval base from which they could command the seas around western Greece. The prosperity that the island had earlier enjoyed waned during the Roman occupation. In AD337, the Roman Empire had grown so large that it was decided to divide it into two and Kefalonia was included in the eastern section which later became Byzantium.

The Byzantine Period (AD337-1267)

From the fifth to seventh centuries, Barbarian tribes from Europe, namely the Vandals and Goths were mounting piratical raids against the Roman Empire. Kefalonia, like other Ionian islands, suffered at their hands as well as from the North African Saracens who too mounted raids. Emperor Heraclius reorganised the administrative themes in 629-634 to create smaller units more able to organise against these attacks. Kefalonia became head of the Theme of Lombardy and was able to use the combined naval force to defend against the Arab raids. Just as the island was regaining some of her old power and prestige, further changes early in the ninth century demoted the island and divided the theme. Fortunes were restored in 887 when Kefalonia again became the administrative head of the Ionian islands and it held this

Above: Ruins of St Marcos church at the Venetian castle, Assos

Below: Ancient ruins at Fiskardo.

position for the next 300 years.

By the eleventh century, events and changes in Europe were posing new threats from the Normans who were pushing into this part of the world. In 1081 the Normans, under Robert Guiscard, took Corfu and his son continued south to capture Kefalonia but failed to overcome the resistance of the islanders. Within three years the Byzantines, backed by a now powerful Venice, was able to recover Corfu and dispel the Norman threat from the region. In return Venice was granted certain trading privileges in the region. There was no lasting peace for the island was again attacked by the Normans and the Genoese. After taking the island in 1147, the Normans were driven out by the Byzantine Emperor Manuel with the help of the Venetians but the island was handed back to the Normans as part of a deal for a peace in 1185. The former corsair, Admiral Margaritus, took control of Kefalonia, Ithaka and Zakynthos and set up his headquarters in St George's castle on Kefalonia.

The Orsini Family (1194-1357)

He was succeeded by Matthios Orsini in 1194 who abolished the Greek orthodox church in favour of Catholicism to gain favour with the pope. The Byzantine Empire finally crumbled as a result of the Fourth Crusade (1202-4). Thanks to help of-

fered to the Crusades, the Venetians gained control of a number of territories along its trade route to the Levant which included the Ionian islands although they did not gain immediate control.

Orsini, once a pirate himself, was nothing if not cunning. By 1209 he decided it was in his best interests to change sides so declared servitude to the Venetians and pacified the Vatican with the promise of a yearly tribute.

In 1258 he was succeeded by his son, Ricardo, but he was no less devious than his father. With the growing power of Theodore Angelos Comnenos, Despot of Epirus, Ricardo took steps to guard his own interests by marrying his son, Ioannes, to Comnenos' daughter. Ioannes Orsini, cast in the same mould, took control on his father's death. Murder and intrigue within the family followed but the Orsinis held on to power up until 1357. In the final years, Ioannes II, who had murdered his brother, renounced the Orsini lineage and adopted the name Ioannes Angelos Comnenos to court popularity. His most serious mistake was to usurp his sisters dowry, the property of her husband, William Tocco, which was half the island of Zakynthos.

The Tocco Dynasty (1357-1479)

In 1335 Ioannes Angelos Comnenos was poisoned by his wife. In

Preceding page: The bell tower at Ag Gerassimos

1357, the King of Naples gave the islands of Kefalonia, Ithaka and Lefkada to Leonard I Tocco. After years of Orsini rule and high taxation, Kefalonia was in a poor state but Leonard adopted a softer policy to advance the welfare and prosperity of the island. This policy survived only as long as Leonard for his successor, Carlo I, already holding land in Epirus, proved to be a greedy and violent ruler until his death in 1429. By this time Venice was engaged in constant running battles with the Turks who were advancing into mainland Greece. Under pressure from the Turks, Carlo II ceded the town of Ioannina to them but they were not appeased and, in 1442, the Turks took control of Zakynthos.

In 1448, Leonard III came to power, the last in a line of five successive Tocco rulers. It was he who returned the rights of the Greek Orthodox church and he also who was forced to yield Kefalonia to the Turks in 1484. The Turks conquered and plundered Kefalonia but their period of rule was short, lasting only until the year 1500.

Venetian Rule (1500-1797)

Back by Spain, Venice launched an attack on Kefalonia in 1500 to dispel the Turks. They laid siege to the castle of St George, captured it and slaughtered the Turkish garrison.

The Venetians were welcomed as liberators by the inhabitants but they merely exchanged one master for another. Rule was invested in noblemen who sought to strengthen the island by encouraging immigrants, a policy fully supported by Venice. In this way the population multiplied, farms organised and a merchant fleet developed for trade. Records show that the population grew from 14,000 in 1548 to around 70,000 in 1655. There were many beneficial aspects of the Venetian rule, they introduced grapes for raisin production, for example, which became a major export product and introduced art and music and generally raised the level of civilisation.

Troubled times still existed, especially in 1537 when Suleiman the Magnificent declared war on Venice. Kefalonia suffered at the hands of Barbarossa, one time pirate then admiral of the Turkish fleet, and again after peace had been concluded in 1540. Ali Pasha too attacked Sami in 1571 inflicting considerable damage but avoided attacking St George's castle, the capital of the island.

The seventeenth century saw the start of a series of earthquakes far worse than the island had previously known. An earthquake in 1634 caused great structural damage and took 540 lives and it was the turn of Lixouri to take the brunt of the 1658 quake.

Venice, a great power throughout this period, was by the start of

Following page: A fresco in a ruined church

the eighteenth century heading into decline. The class system of rule introduced by the Venetians brought its own problems on Kefalonia. Powerful noble families attracted bands of followers which created trouble and erupted into civil war in 1755 involving the Metaxa and the Anninos families. Venice was powerless to intervene and Kefalonia was ready to court a new protector.

Exhausted by its long struggles, Venice was finally defeated by Napoleon in 1797 and Kefalonia, like the other Ionian islands became a French possession.

French and Russian Masters (1797-1809)

The French were greeted with excitement and they responded by outlawing the now hated aristocratic system of rule. In the following year, disaster overtook the French fleet at the Battle of Abukir after which they were forced to yield the Ionian islands to the Russians and the Turks. First action of the Russo-Turkish regime was to restore the aristocratic system of administration. In a joint declaration by the Russian and Turkish admirals, the Ionian islands were joined to become one nation, the Septinsular Republic. Fourteen delegates made up the governing senate and eventually a constitution was drawn up which acknowledged the fact that the Republic was a Russian protectorate.

By the treaty of Tilsit, in 1807, the Ionian islands were ceded back to France who were again greeted warmly. Once again the French occupation was doomed to be short lived but this time the threat came from Britain.

The British Rule (1809-1864)

In 1809, Britain mounted a blockade of the Ionian islands as part of the war against Napoleon and, on 19 September of the same year, hoisted the British flag over Zakynthos castle. Kefalonia and Ithaka quickly surrendered and the British installed provisional governments. The Treaty of Paris in 1815 recognised the United States of the Ionian islands and decreed that it become a British protectorate. Colonel Charles Philippe de Bosset, a Swiss serving in the British army, became provisional governor between 1810 and 1814. During those years he was credited with many public works including the Drapano causeway bridge at Argo-stoli. Thomas Maitland, the first Lord High Commissioner in 1815, devised a constitution for the Ionians which concentrated power in his own hands. Although he initiated many public works to improve the infrastructure and protect and encourage trade, he was disliked for his autocratic ways. Resistance groups started to form although much of their energy in the early years was directed to support-

Preceding page: The ruins of Ag Fanentes Monastery

ing the Greeks in their revolution against the Turks.

By 1848 the resistance movement was gaining strength and turning against the British. There were skirmishes with the British army in Argostoli and Lixouri which led to some relaxation of the laws including a greater freedom for the press. Union with Greece was now a declared aim and, by 1850, a growing restlessness resulted in still more skirmishes which were put down with violence. Kefalonia, along with the other Ionian islands, were ceded to Greece as a gesture of goodwill when the British-backed Prince William of Denmark became King George I of the Hellenes.

The period of British rule had many positive aspects. Many of the island's roads were constructed, a new Ionian Academy formed, educational standards improved and greater prosperity enjoyed.

Union with Greece (1864)

After union, Kefalonians had greater freedom of movement and, with repeated earthquakes around the middle of the century, a great wave of emigration commenced to other Greek cities or to other counties. Farming decreased on the island but shipping remained important. Trade unionism appeared in the early decades after union with Greece and political movements started, particularly Socialism.

Out and About

Good Beach Guide

A day out on a different beach provides a refreshing change and the purpose of this guide is to help with choices. It is not intended to be a comprehensive list but includes only those beaches with good features which reward the effort of getting there. Sandy beaches are selected in the main but outstandingly good shingle beaches are also included. Refer to the map on pages 22-23 for locations and for ease of reference they are listed in clockwise order starting from Argostoli. Further details may be found by consulting the car tours.

Lassi: this is the name given to the peninsula which encloses Argostoli bay but since the development of tourism the area of Lassi seems to have expanded to encompass much of the coastline running southwards towards the airport. The following four beaches which lie close together are now promoted as Lassi.

P138

Kalamia beach: the most northerly of the Lassi beaches, part way up the headland. It has a narrow stretch of grey sand with a band of fine shingle at the waters edge but set in small, picturesque bay bounded by white cliffs to the south. Access by foot from the road down grass track. Facilities include beach beds and umbrellas which are cheaper here than most other beaches on the island, also small bar.

Gradakia beach: small but deep inlet with grey sand and a clear sea. Beach beds, umbrellas and a bar provide all the facilities necessary.

Makrys Gialos: situated a short walk down from the main road, this is probably the most popular beach along this coast. A fine, long stretch of golden sand although without great depth. Plenty of facilities including beach furniture, bars, tavernas and a good range of water sports; good for families.

Platys Gialos: Similar in character and sand quality to Makrys Gialos but smaller. It has similar facilities but here includes changing rooms and showers; also good for families. The inviting spit of sand running out to a small, rocky headland just to the south, known as Tourkopodaro, is part of the white Rocks Hotel complex.

Lourdas beach: unless resident in the area, this one is not easy to reach without a car. A long stretch of fine silver sand with just a little shingle enclosed by a wide bay. There is very little development around so the beach tends to be quiet but there are tavernas to hand and some beach furniture; limited water sports.

Skala: Good sandy beach which is both long and deep, unlikely to get too crowded. Plenty of facilities to hand, some water sports and good for families.

Preceding pages: Fiskardo

Poros: not the best beach, mainly shingle and quite narrow, but one of the liveliest for water sports with a whole gamut of activities available from pedaloes to paragliding. Good facilities close on hand.

Anti Samos: located 3km (2miles) south of Sami and accessed by a road surfaced almost all the way. A sweep of white pebbles lapped by a violet sea in picturesque setting. Beautiful beach, clear waters but minimal facilities, just sun beds, umbrellas and drinks.

Myrtos beach: Spectacular beach of fine white sand and shingle nestling into steep cliffs. It is a real sun trap and gets very hot. Accessed from the main road high above by a road surfaced for much of the way but track for the last section. Facilities limited to a beach bar offering sun beds and umbrellas.

P 61
Lepeda beach: located just south of Lixouri, this small cove has a beach of golden sand. Attractive setting and complete with all the essential facilities.

A Day Out in Argostoli

A stroll around Argostoli will easily fill half a day, including visits to the museums. The large main square is a magnet for the evening 'volta' when locals and visitors alike mingle to socialise and watch the world go by. Oleanders add splashes of vibrant colour to the streets in summer where shaded outdoor cafés provide cooling drinks. Most of the main points of interest are close to the centre but the lighthouse lies two kilometres out of town along the peninsula.

The main points of interest are; The Archaeological Museum; Korgialenios History and Folklore Museum; Central Square; Lithostroto pedestrianised shopping street; Fruit and vegetable market; Fish sellers along the quayside; Drapano Bridge; Katavothres swallow holes and the lighthouse of Ag Theodori.

Argostoli sits in the shelter of the Koutavos lagoon, a natural harbour within the larger Gulf of Argostoli. The town itself lies along the peninsula which separates the lagoon from the gulf and is sheltered from sight of the open sea by a chain of low hills. Once the harbour for Mycenaean Krani, whose remains are scattered in the hills to the east of Argostoli, it later provided anchorage for Saracens and pirates who regularly raided the island.

By the time links with the Byzantine empire were broken and the island passed to Venetian control in 1204, it was under the iron grip of the Orsini family. By this time, the capital of Kefalonia had already been moved from Pali (near Lixouri) to the castle of St George, 5km (3 miles) south of present day Argostoli. A combination of administrative movement between the Ionian Islands and further afield plus a growing trade in raisins brought an increase in shipping to the harbour.

Sunseeker Tips

1. BEACH BEDS
The cost of hiring sun beds and umbrellas is overpriced and seems to climb each year. The total cost over a full two week holiday can be quite significant. A full day's rate is charged even if the loungers are used for only a couple of hours. One alternative is to buy beach umbrellas and air beds which are freely available in the shops. Their cost will be recovered in just two or three days and, if luggage space is tight when departing, it is no loss if they are passed on to some newly arrived holidaymakers.

2. BARS WITH POOLS
Watch out for one of the growing number of purpose built bars with swimming pools which offer all the facilities free to customers, including free use of sun beds and parasols, providing drinks and food are bought from the bar. Prices are not usually elevated and many of these sell good value bar snacks. It is a growing market and a number of hotels are following the trend and also offer their swimming pool and facilities free on the same basis.

3. FRAPPE
Hot drinks lose their appeal when the weather is very hot and a more suitable drink for coffee fans is iced coffee or frappe. It is very easy to make and self catering visitors can put one together in a trice. Plastic frappe makers, nothing more than a plastic container with lid, can be bought cheaply but an empty coffee jar with lid is ideal. For one cup add a normal measure of instant coffee, ice cubes, milk and sugar if taken, and a cup of chilled water.

Shake vigorously to dissolve the coffee, around 30 seconds, pour into a glass and it should have a good head of froth. Drink through a straw, for some reason it tastes better.

4. POST CARDS
To speed up the delivery of post cards, put them into an airmail envelope before posting. Postal rate is the same and they are delivered as letters which means a few days instead of a couple of weeks. Envelopes (*fakellos*) can be bought cheaply at stationers.

5. MUSEUMS AND ARCHAEOLOGICAL SITES
Except for private museums, there is no charge on Sundays for entry to museums and archaeological sites throughout Greece.

A Note of Warning
Care is needed on the beach to avoid stings from jelly fish and, in rocky regions, from sea urchins. If you are unlucky enough to have a brush with the latter then it is important to ensure that all the spines are properly removed. Wearing beach shoes will give your feet some protection from stings of this nature (see also Mosquitoes, page 132).

Below: Anti Samos beach

This increased traffic led, in 1560, to a basic dock being built where present day Argostoli stands; then no more than a clutch of fishermen's cottages. Administrative control remained in the castle though, whilst commercial activity developed apace in the area of the harbour, a situation which hampered the growth of the islands economy. In 1753, a delegate was sent to Venice to ask that Argostoli be made the administrative centre of the island. After six years of petitioning this request was finally granted and, in 1759, Argostoli became the capital of Kefalonia.

Before the turn of the eighteenth century, Argostoli had developed into a town of order with elegant mansions and graceful bell-towers. During the early nineteenth century, the first governor under British administration, the Swiss Philippe de Bosset (1810-1814), a colonel in the British army, carried out further improvements to the islands infrastructure. Under his governorship the many-arched Drapano causeway bridge was built and he also built roads to Sami and Assos. Colonel Sir Charles Napier, a later governor appointed in 1821, continued with a programme of road building, erected public buildings and created a public park in Argostoli which was named Napier Park. Napier was obviously at ease amongst the Greeks of Kefalonia as this entry in his diary from 1825 shows:-

'Now I am once more amongst the merry Greeks who are worth all other nations put together. I like to see to hear them. I like their fun, their good humour, their paddy ways, for they are very like Irishmen. All their bad habits are Venetian. Their wit, their eloquence, their good nature are their own.'

The wealthier residents of Argostoli enjoyed a high standard of living and cultural activity, enhanced by the installation of electricity in 1908. Decline came with the World Wars of the twentieth century and Greece's civil war afterwards. At the time of the earthquakes of August 1953, the town was beginning to return to a more settled existence.

After the devastating earthquake of 12 August 1953, not much of Argostoli was left standing. Gone were most of the graceful mansions and public buildings leaving streets piled with rubble. Many Kefalonians chose to emigrate but, with the help of other European countries, a rebuilding programme was set in motion. Little thought was given to style initially, it being more important to rebuild homes and administrative buildings as quickly as possible. Efforts to re-establish some of its earlier style and grace, can be seen in more recent buildings like the Theatre and restoration of some older buildings.

Despite the loss of its former Venetian ambience, Argostoli is a friendly and thriving town with a charm of its own.

Start out in the ambient surrounds of the central square which becomes the focal point of summer evening activity in the town. Traffic is banned and Greek families come to enjoy the café atmosphere of the spacious square, where children can play in safety. Facing the square is the nondescript Town Hall building, a victim of the hurried reconstruction programme after the earthquake of 1953.

South from the square is the **Ar-** **chaeological Museum**, typical of an uninspired museum design and presentation all too often encountered throughout Greece. Fortunately, the exhibits themselves are an interesting collection of Mycenaean, Hellenistic and Roman finds from the island; much depleted now as an earlier museum and many exhibits were destroyed in 1953. Visitors are greeted by male and female skeletons, a third century burial from Kambothekrata. There is also a fine Roman bronze head from the third century AD and, of particular appeal, a sculpted plaque and disc found in the Melissani Cave and thought to be connected with the god Pan cult. Excellent exhibits, but a lack of variety and indifferent display reduces their impact.

Open: Tuesday to Sunday 8.30am-3pm; closed Monday and holidays. Admission charge.

✳ The bright façade of the **Kefalos Theatre** draws the eye up right on leaving the Archaeological Museum. It has only recently been rebuilt after the original theatre was destroyed by German incendiaries in 1943. Founded in 1857 by public subscription, in return for which each founding member owned a box, the theatre opened its doors in 1859. Music and drama figured highly in the cultural life of the Ionian islands as a whole and touring companies regularly came over from Italy. A production of 'La Traviata', with scenery painted by a stage designer from the 'Fenice Opera House' in Venice, was presented on the opening night. The theatre was also used increasingly for dramatic works in Greek. Theatre activity is usually at its height between October and the start of Lent; for current productions enquire at the Tourist Office. Head up along the left side of the Theatre to the Korgialenios Library and Museum.

Korgialenios Cultural and His- **torical Museum**, situated beneath the library of the same name, was established by Mrs Eleni Kosmetatou in 1960 and opened in 1966. This enterprising lady has gathered together a superb collection of artefacts, mainly relating to nineteenth-century life but not exclusively. Exhibits are kept in pristine condition and are thoughtfully displayed, with explanations in English. Exquisite examples of lace work, costumes, household utensils and tools etc reveal the high standard of living and culture enjoyed by the wealthy inhabitants. There is also a folkloric room, a small impressive ecclesiastical display and a riveting photographic record of more recent history. The collection is a shining example of how a museum should be laid out and interestingly presented. A definite must for visitors young or old.

Open: Monday to Saturday 9am-

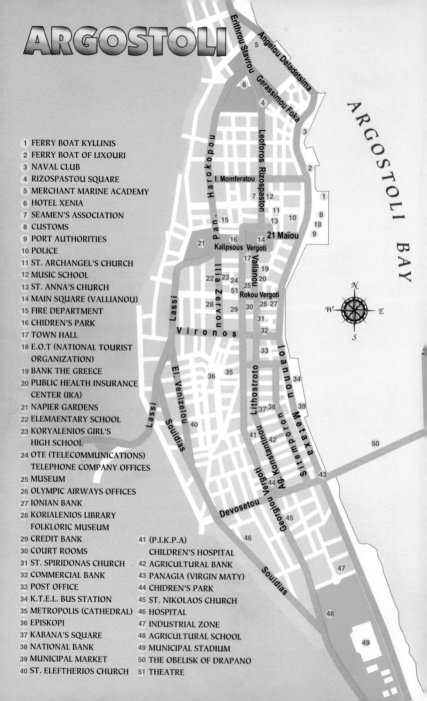

ARGOSTOLI

1. FERRY BOAT KYLLINIS
2. FERRY BOAT OF LIXOURI
3. NAVAL CLUB
4. RIZOSPASTOU SQUARE
5. MERCHANT MARINE ACADEMY
6. HOTEL XENIA
7. SEAMEN'S ASSOCIATION
8. CUSTOMS
9. PORT AUTHORITIES
10. POLICE
11. ST. ARCHANGEL'S CHURCH
12. MUSIC SCHOOL
13. ST. ANNA'S CHURCH
14. MAIN SQUARE (VALLIANOU)
15. FIRE DEPARTMENT
16. CHIDREN'S PARK
17. TOWN HALL
18. E.O.T (NATIONAL TOURIST
    ORGANIZATION)
19. BANK THE GREECE
20. PUBLIC HEALTH INSURANCE
    CENTER (IKA)
21. NAPIER GARDENS
22. ELEMAENTARY SCHOOL
23. KORYALENIOS GIRL'S
    HIGH SCHOOL
24. OTE (TELECOMMUNICATIONS)
    TELEPHONE COMPANY OFFICES
25. MUSEUM
26. OLYMPIC AIRWAYS OFFICES
27. IONIAN BANK
28. KORIALENIOS LIBRARY
    FOLKLORIC MUSEUM
29. CREDIT BANK
30. COURT ROOMS
31. ST. SPIRIDONAS CHURCH
32. COMMERCIAL BANK
33. POST OFFICE
34. K.T.E.L. BUS STATION
35. METROPOLIS (CATHEDRAL)
36. EPISKOPI
37. KABANA'S SQUARE
38. NATIONAL BANK
39. MUNICIPAL MARKET
40. ST. ELEFTHERIOS CHURCH

41. (P.I.K.P.A)
    CHILDREN'S HOSPITAL
42. AGRICULTURAL BANK
43. PANAGIA (VIRGIN MATY)
44. CHIDREN'S PARK
45. ST. NIKOLAOS CHURCH
46. HOSPITAL
47. INDUSTRIAL ZONE
48. AGRICULTURAL SCHOOL
49. MUNICIPAL STADIUM
50. THE OBELISK OF DRAPANO
51. THEATRE

The Earthquake of 1953

The Kefalonians were not completely unprepared for the earthquake of 12 August 1953, only for the extent of the devastation. A couple of strong tremors during the preceding days had alerted the population to the danger. So much so, that many abandoned their homes to live in the open. The strongest tremor, which registered 7.5 on the Richter scale, swept up through Zakynthos and Kefalonia. It veered off before reaching the northern tip of the island at Fiskardo, which escaped relatively unscathed. An eye-witness account tells of the rippling effect of the tremor's approach. Of how he looked round to see people dancing like puppets and then suddenly found himself being tossed helplessly about.

Argostoli and much of the island was reduced to rubble. It is reckoned that 85 per cent of the buildings were totally demolished. Fortunately, loss of life was limited because of the warning tremors beforehand. The British were first on the scene to help the inhabitants by organising shelters and restoring some of the infrastructure. At first, the inhabitants were suspicious of high buildings and the square, red-tile roofed bungalow type of house stems from that time. All building specifications since then, have to withstand earthquakes of well over 8 on the Richter Scale.

Earthquakes have always been a problem in this part of the world. One reason why Kefalonia has little to show of the Byzantine influence is the result of earthquakes during the seventeenth century. Damage was even inflicted in the nineteenth century which resulted in some rebuilding. In fact, between August 1953 and April 1954 a further 3,000 tremors were recorded. Minor tremors are a fact of every day life but mostly go unremarked by visitors unused to such phenomena.

A sobering photographic record of pre and post earthquake Argostoli is clearly displayed in the Historical and Folklore Museum within the Korgialenios Library, which is situated on the road behind the Theatre.

2pm; closed Sunday. Admission charge.

✻ The **Korgialenios Library** was founded in 1924 with a bequest from Marinos Korgialenios, destroyed in 1953 and since rebuilt. It houses some 46,000 volumes and historical documents relating to the history of Kefalonia. From the library, return down past the Archaeological Museum to turn right into pedestrianised Lithostroto.

Narrow **Lithostroto** was supposedly part of the first area to be built and inhabited in Argostoli and named so because this was the first street to be paved in stone. It has always been the shopping heart of town and is lined with a selection of boutiques, the post office and shops selling a range of goods, especially souvenirs. Along this street can also be found the **Church of Ag Spiridon** (Corfu's patron saint). A procession leaves from here every 12 August to commemorate the 1953 earthquake. Further along is the Roman Catholic **Church of Ag Nikolaos** behind which is located the 1957 **Greek Orthodox Cathedral**. The forlorn looking bell-tower, on the right beyond the post office, was built by the Venetians in the eighteenth century when the small square opposite was a lively spot called the 'Piazzetta'. Take a left turn to reach the harbour front.

Emerge on the harbour front close to the Bus Station and the major shopping area for the islanders. Here are located, the larger supermarkets, bakers, butchers and an excellent fruit and vegetable market.

The market appears to remain open all day every day in season and the produce is fresh and reasonably priced. Along the quayside to the north fishermen sell directly to the customer, their catch, an assortment of familiar and often unusual fish, displayed for selection. Most local shopping activity takes place early morning and evenings of late shopping days. Views stretch out beyond the lagoon to the hills on the far side, now reached across the Drapano causeway bridge which slices the lagoon into two parts.

The **Drapano Bridge** was built at ✻ the instigation of the then British governor, Colonel Philippe de Bosset in 1813. This link with the coast opposite was greeted with suspicion at first, the townspeople not too happy that unruly elements in villages on the far side of the lagoon would have easier access to Argostoli. Bridge building was made easier by the shallow water at this point and the first bridge, on wooden trestles, took only fifteen days to erect. It was replaced with one made of interlocking stones, without the use of cement, three years later and widened in 1842. The obelisk halfway across commemorates the date of the bridge and Colonel de Bosset. An alternative road now skirts the top end of the lagoon, passing close to the site of ancient Krani, but involves a detour of a few kilometres.

Palm trees and seats line the black and white pebble patterned promenade, which separates the road from the quay. At the northern end is the tourist office and the departure point for ferries to Lixouri. Beyond, the road does a 4km (2½ miles) loop round the peninsula to the resort area of Lassi, which is actually only a fifteen minute walk over the hill from Argostoli. A different route back to the centre from the Lixouri ferry port is to head inland to Leoforos Rizospaston. This wide spacious avenue lined with oleander and palm trees leads directly back to the square. Alternatively, continue along the loop road for around 1km (½ mile), to see one of the island's more unusual features. Away from the main holiday season the road is fairly quiet and wends along the peninsula close to the shore for most of the way.

❋ On the shore behind a night club and restaurant is the **Katavothres**, swallow holes down which seawater use to disappear in volumes but not since the earthquake. See page 51 for further details. Changes seem to have occurred though and less water flows these days. A waterwheel is the only reminder of a nineteenth-century watermill which once stood on the site and, before World War II, the water power was harnessed to fuel an electricity plant. The lighthouse at the end of the peninsula is reached in a further kilometre.

❋ The **Ag Theodori lighthouse** was constructed in 1829 under the Napier administration. A round Doric style building, it was destroyed in the earthquake of 1875 and rebuilt to the original plan. This is a good spot to enjoy watching the sun set. Either return to Argostoli by the same route or continue round the peninsula to Lassi.

A DAY IN FISKARDO

Tucked away on the northern tip of the island, Fiskardo is a picture postcard harbour set in a natural bay. Red-roofed pastel coloured houses crowd the waterfront looking onto an azure blue bay full of dancing yachts. A table on the quayside here is all that is needed to feel at peace with the world. If there is an urge to wander then the main things to see and enjoy include: the charm of the harbour; a wander around the village to see some Venetian and neo Classic pre-earthquake houses, the only ones on the island; inspect the old Byzantine church on the headland; see the excavations of a Roman site showing sarcophagi; enjoy a swim from the small shingle beach nearby; visit the church of Panagia.

Fiskardo usually features on the island tours offered by the tour operators but it is worth more time than a brief stop. Buses leave Argostoli on weekdays, usually at 10am and 2pm, bound for Fiskardo and return at 5pm. Ferry boat from Fiskardo to Sami offers a more romantic way to travel back. The boat calls in at Ithaka but only to load and it is straight off again. Check the return bus times from Sami to Argostoli to ensure that the programme dovetails.

There was a period in history, before the advent of roads, that remote Fiskardo was popularly believed not

Eating Out in Argostoli

Good eating can be enjoyed in many resorts around the island but the selection of restaurants is particularly good in Argostoli town which offers some of the best eating in the Ionian islands. Here are a few recommendations to start with but there are other restaurants equally good. The comparative prices are indicated by $ for cheap to $$$ for expensive.

PATSURAS: at the northern end of Rizospaston street which leads out of the main square. A different selection of good Greek dishes every night, diners are invited into the kitchen to make their selection. The house wine is good too, ask for *krasi dopio*. $

THE CAPTAIN'S TABLE: also on Rizospaston street near the main square. Good food from an interesting menu. $$

AGROBELI; also on Rizospaston street, next to Captain's Table. Small taverna with good Greek dishes and a good house wine. $

CYPRUS TAVERN: 1 Lavranga street, just out of the south-east corner of the main square. Specialises in mezedes, lots of small plates. Excellent food and should suit big appetites. $$$

STO PSITO: 8 M. Anninou street, three blocks behind the theatre. Intimate garden atmosphere with an interesting and varied menu. $$

THE COTTAGE (Kalyva), just above the main square. Popular taverna with varied Greek menu. $$

Above: Argostoli with the Drapano bridge obelisk

Below: Fiskardo harbour

to be part of Kefalonia but to be on an altogether different island. Perhaps it was this isolation which attracted settlers throughout the ages. These ages start very early for Fiskardo, as early as prehistoric times, and the whole area is littered with archaeological evidence in the form of flint axe-heads, ridged knives and similar tools. During Mycenaean times, Fiskardo was subordinate to Sami when it was known simply as Panormos, a descriptive term meaning a 'bay for all' indicating a safe bay for shipping. A stronghold built with massive polygonal stonework in typical Mycenaean style exists at Pyrgos which lies in the mountains south of Fiskardo, near Plagia, and coins found there suggest occupation in Roman times. Excavations now in hand in Fiskardo itself show a burial ground from the Roman period right by the sea edge. Much of the area around Fiskardo has been declared an archaeological site which means that no new building is permitted.

The ruins of the Byzantine church standing on the headland tell of an organised community in Byzantine times and this ruin is now unique on the island since other monuments from this period have been destroyed by the various earthquakes endured from the seventeenth century onwards. Kefalonia has suffered many aggressors over the centuries but one particular historical event in 1081 led to a change of name for Panormos. This is when the Normans, under Robert Guiscard, attacked the Ionian islands. Robert

headed for Corfu and managed to take it while his son continued south to capture Kefalonia. When it was clear that the resistance on Kefalonia was successfully keeping his son at bay, Robert brought reinforcements and landed at Panormos. The elder Guiscard became ill with fever and died which proved fortunate for Kefalonia as the siege was promptly aborted. Panormos was renamed Guiscardo which over the centuries changed in stages to Fiskardo.

Except for traffic heading to the ferry, cars are kept out of the village centre and made to park just outside. It is but a short walk down to the quay which is the heart of the village and the best place to start a tour. Expect a lively atmosphere on summer days with yachts constantly coming and going, people eating beneath the sun shades on the quayside with others browsing in the tourists shops. This you can expect to see in any harbour town on the island but the particular character of Fiskardo is provided by the pastel coloured nineteenth and early twentieth century neo-Classical houses which form the backdrop. For some reason, Fiskardo escaped major damage from earthquakes which so badly affected the rest of the island. Most new houses built this century conformed to the traditional style even before 1975 when the government decreed that Fiskardo be preserved as a traditional village. Strict building regulations to maintain this neo-Classical style are now imposed. Only the older houses in the village show any Venetian elements in their design.

A stepped street at the southern corner of the harbour leads up to the church of Panagia (Holy Mother), the village's only church. Standing on this site originally was a small Byzantine church which, in 1673, was converted into a monastery. Restoration was needed after the earthquake of 1767 but the monastery continued in operation until 1911 housing up to around six nuns. The ikconostasis inside the church is highly ornate and worth seeing but the church is mostly kept locked so it will be necessary to enquire locally for the keyholder. Celebrations for the saints day take place on 8 September.

Wandering further south around the headland leads to the small shingle beach and on the way there is a view into excavations taking place by the edge of the sea. A number of sarcophagi are on view from the Roman period which were discovered only recently during the construction of the adjacent taverna. Other Roman remains are thought to lie in this area. The beach is just a little further on and the sparklingly clear water is very inviting.

Ferries for Ithaka or Lefkas leave from a reserved area at the north end of the harbour. Walking beyond here heads onto Fournias, the headland where the ruins of the Byzantine church can be seen. There seems to be a maze of footpaths leading up to the church but with the ruins standing on the highest point and clearly in view, picking a route through presents no difficulty. There is speculation that before Christianity a temple to Apollo stood on this spot and, following the island's conversion towards the end of the first century, it was replaced by a church. It is believed that this Byzantine church was built originally in the sixth century. The most impressive parts visible today are the two towers guarding the church entrance which illustrate the dual role of the church in troubled times as a safe refuge as well as a place of worship. Also on the headland is an engraved rock known as the Throne of Queen ✳ Fiskardo. This ancient place of worship is believed to be a sacrificial altar. Towards the end of Fournias headland is a Venetian lighthouse.

A DAY IN LIXOURI

Lixouri is the second largest town on Kefalonia and lies on the Paliki peninsula. Built around a port, it is a modern town with more of a working atmosphere than Argostoli but worth a visit to absorb the atmosphere which is perhaps more Greek than anywhere else on the island. Things to see and do include: enjoy a ferry ride; explore the town; visit the museum of ikons; swim from Lepeda beach.

The easiest way to get to Lixouri from Argostoli is to take the car ferry which plies back and forth to a regular timetable. It leaves hourly from Argostoli on the half hour, starting at 8.30am, and returns from Lixouri on the hour, last boat 10pm.

Lixouri is the capital of the Paliki peninsula which is the most in-

The Monk Seal

The sea between Kefalonia and Ithaka is frequented by the rare and endangered monk seal, Monachus monachus which thrives in the warm waters of the Mediterranean and Atlantic off the coast of North Africa.

Mentioned by Homer, they were much more prolific in the ancient world but have been disturbed over recent centuries by the loss of breeding habitats and by conflict with fishermen. This rather shy animal takes refuge in caves and remote places out of sight of man to give birth to young which is usually a single pup. Tourist development along the coast and increased leisure activity around the sea shores have seriously interfered with the regular haunts of this species.

The monk seal lives on fish and octopus but, with ever diminishing supplies, it has brought them into direct competition with fishermen. Too many times in the past has the conflict been resolved simply by killing the seal, especially when they get caught up in nets. Now the emphasis is strictly on conservation and the World Wildlife Fund supports a project to conserve a small population of these seals which is known to exist in the area around Kefalonia, Ithaka and Lefkas.

Below: Katavothres, Argostoli

tensely cultivated part of Kefalonia. Olives, vines, citrus fruits, strawberries, melons, figs and vegetables are amongst the regular crops and all this farming activity is reflected in the character of Lixouri. It is the produce from this area which fills the markets in Argostoli.

Organised settlements have been present on this peninsula from Mycenaean times and the ancient city of Pali was located on the hill just to the north of the present location of Lixouri. Little remains now to be seen of Pali since much of the stone was reused when the town resettled. The date of resettlement is not known with certainty but Lixouri enters historical records around 1534.

The destructive earthquake of 1953 effectively demolished Lixouri, as it did many of the other places on the island. It was rebuilt on modern, clean lines with wide roads and streets well decked with trees and flowers. Greeting visitors at the harbour as they arrive by ferry is a statue of Andreas Laskaratus (1811-1901) dressed in long coat with top hat in hand. He was a poet and intellectual who became one of Lixouri's most famous sons. Behind lies the large main square which is the hub of the town in all respects. It is where the menfolk sit in shaded cafes drinking coffee, setting the world to right or simply idling away time with the help of a komboloi. Usually a string of wood, plastic or metal beads, komboloi are the Greek's own form of worry beads used by men to relax from the stresses and strains of everyday life. It seems to be a preserve of men and women are rarely seen using them. Partially wrapped around the fingers of hand, the beads are revolved in a flicking motion but there are several techniques of worrying which are surprisingly difficult to imitate for the untrained. Komboloi are thought to have developed from the Turkish rosary which has ninety nine pearls representing the names of Allah. This is clearly too unwieldy to use as a toy so the Greeks reduced the number to 13 or 15, or sometimes 17. For the Greeks it is a toy or a lucky charm and has no religious significance whatsoever. Surrounded by tavernas and cafés, the spacious square is the place to eat in Lixouri.

The **library and museum** is located on the coastal side, in an old mansion which survived the earthquake. The mansion originally belonged to the Lakovatos family but was donated by them to use as a museum. It now houses a valuable library of up to 20,000 books, some very old, which have been donated from various sources. Ikons and religious artefacts figure prominently in the museum section.

Nearby is the **Church of Ag Haralambos**, named after the patron saint of the town. Haralambos was a priest from Asia Minor in AD198 who survived the Christian persecution despite his ripe old age which was said to be over a hundred. His

Preceding page: Ruins of a Byzantine church, Fiskardo

remains were kept in a monastery in Meteora and presented to the town only in 1952. The sculptured figure decorating the bell tower of the church represents the plague and is there because Ag Haralambos is believed to have saved the town from it.

Wandering to the south of town leads to a number of small shingle beaches but the best is **Lepeda** which lies 3km (2 miles) south of town. The simplest option is to use a taxi and arrange a time of collection. Picturesque Lepeda beach of rich golden sand sits within a cove bounded by a rocky outcrop to the north. On hand is a small ouzeri supplying drinks and snacks and there are sun beds and shades to hire.

For those with transport or prepared to use a taxi, there are a number of other beaches to visit at the south end of the Paliki peninsula, around 8km (5miles) south of Lix-ouri. The most distant is Akrotiri on the southernmost tip. Akrotiri beach lies in a small bay and has a deep crescent of golden sand, very natural and quiet but no facilities. Nearby Kounopetra has a small harbour for fishing boats but nowhere to swim except from the rocks. East of Akro-tiri is the beach marked on maps as Xi but also known as Ammoudia. Here the Sahara-red sand contrasts sharply with the putty-white cliffs behind which it makes it hard to appreciate that this is natural and not a man-made beach. It has a seasonal taverna and a hotel on hand but is clearly a developing area. Sun beds

and umbrellas can be hired on the beach. East again of Ammoudia is Megas Lakos, the last of the beaches on the southern coast. Megas Lakos offers a narrow stretch of golden sand which extends towards and into Ammoudia. It has a taverna and some seasonal accommodation but little else.

A TRIP TO ITHAKA

Ithaka (Ithaki in Greek and Thaki to the locals), is the fifth largest island in the Ionian group. It is almost two mountainous islands connected by a narrow neck of land and lies a few kilometres east of northern Kefalonia. Vathy, the capital, and Perahori village lie in the southern part whilst a cluster of villages in the north form the other most populated area. This is the reputed home of the hero in Homer's *Odyssey*, Odysseus, King of Ithaka. See box page 66. The island's barren mountains leave little space for habitation but picturesque harbours and sleepy villages have gained a toehold in fertile pockets. Most of what there is to see can be visited in the course of a day trip and should include: Vathy, Museum and Cathedral with fine ikonostasis; Cave of the Nymphs; Kathara Monastery and Anogi; Pilikata Archaeological Museum; Exogi and Platrithias hill villages; Frikes and Kioni coastal villages.

There are a number of boats daily to Ithaka from Fiskardo and Sami plus one from Ag Efimia. Check sailing times with a local shipping office or travel agent as the times given

Above: Lixouri

Below: Kounopetra harbour

Above: Ammoudia beach. It looks man-made, but it isn't!

Below: Vathy, the capital of Ithaka

here are liable to seasonal and yearly change, by way of example: Fiskardo to Frikes 9.30am and 10.30am; Fiskardo to Pisso Aetos 12noon and 6.45pm; Sami to Pisso Aetos 6am, 7.45am and 2.30pm; Ag Efimia to Pisso Aetos 9.15am.

Organised trips include a tour of the island but independent travellers with a hire car have more flexibility. Most of the ferries carry cars but always check. Foot passengers need to choose their port of entry carefully. Frikes is a small picturesque fishing village, 3km from Stavros the main village in the north of the island. There are facilities in Frikes and it is possible to walk to the surrounding villages. It is also possible to hire a taxi; ask at one of the tavernas. Pisso Aetos is out in the middle of nowhere; a narrow strip of shingle beach and a jetty. Taxis sometimes meet the boat but not reliably so and it is a long walk to the nearest town of Vathy. Those taking their own car can make the most of the island in a day by sailing from Fiskardo to Frikes and returning Pisso Aetos to Sami.

The island was first inhabited between 4000-3000BC as finds displayed in the Pilikata Museum suggest. By around 1500BC the whole island was inhabited and, along with Kefalonia, developed into an important Mycenaean centre. In Homer's *Odyssey*, Ithaka is supposed to have been ruled by Odysseus around 1200BC. A later decline in population, especially in the south, is attributed to lack of fertile soil but the north remained populated and cultivated. The island flourished as a commercial station from 734BC, when it was on the shipping route between Corinth and its colony of Corfu. Activity was centred in the north part of the island and the port town of Jerusalem, in the Bay of Polis. The town has long since vanished beneath the waves, abandoned and then finally sunk during an earthquake in AD967. During the Roman occupation Ithaka became part of the Roman province but their control crumbled after AD337 when the Roman Empire was split into two.

Under Norman rule and then the Orsini Family, Ithaka's history continues following a course similar to that of neighbouring Kefalonia. It was sacked by the Turks at the end of the fifteenth century who took hostages to sell as slaves. Many who were left fled, seriously depleting the population. When they resumed control in AD1500, the Venetians encouraged re-population of the island by offering grants of land and exemption from taxes.

In the sixteenth century Vathy became the capital of the island. Poor soil meant little cultivable land so the islanders turned to the sea for a living. By the seventeenth century, the island's fleet was being used for trade with Europe and for attacks against the Turks. At the time of union with Greece in 1864, Ithaka had a sound reputation in commerce and shipping. Unfortunately Ithaka, like its neighbour Kefalonia, has suffered earthquake damage over the centuries. This, coupled with little sustainable land, has led many to emigrate although a growth in tourism is reversing this trend and encouraging some islanders to return.

Pisso Aetos is nothing more than a sweep of bay with a jetty. Aetos means 'eagle' in Greek. The narrow beach is used by swimmers and the jetty shared by local fishermen and a 'Kantina' for drinks and snacks. A road winds up the hill from the harbour to a saddle, the site of ancient Alalkomenes and on the hill above that of an acropolis; known locally as 'Odysseus' Castle'. There are remains of a Cyclopean wall and Hellenistic cemetery. Schliemann excavated a Mycenaean tomb here. The citadel dates from 1400BC and was destroyed by the same earthquake which felled Delphi in 400BC. Lack of funding has led to spasmodic excavation of this site, which links to the four ancient cities on Kefalonia. A Sanctuary to Apollo, the foundations of a temple and more recently an irrigation fountain, apparently the first of its type discovered in Greece, have been revealed. Continue on over the hill to join the main road where a right turn leads to Vathy, the capital.

Watch out for a road off right, signposted to the **Cave of the Nymphs**. This starts off as surfaced road which reverts to track as it wends for 2½km (1½ miles) into the countryside. Follow the signs to a small parking area below a small green hut on the hillside. A paved path leads uphill the short way to the hut and opening into the cave. The cave lies at an altitude of 190m (623ft) and is entered via an iron gate, which is usually unlocked. Here is where Odysseus is said to have hidden gifts from Alkinoos, king of the Phaeacians who lived on Scherie (Corfu). Mere mortals enter through this northern gate whilst the gods had exclusive use of a southern entrance. Once through the narrow opening, steps lead down into a deeper pit-like cave lit by a shaft of light. Excavations here in 1805 revealed pottery, clay figurines and a marble base for a statue.

Back on the main road, continue towards Vathy past the islands main beach of **Dexia**. This is thought to be the Homeric cove of Forkis (named after the Old Man of the Sea) and the spot where the Phaeacians landed the sleeping Odysseus on his return to Ithaka. **Vathy** (deep) is the main harbour and capital of Ithaka, enclosed by hills and edging the far end of the horseshoe shaped inlet. Its pastel coloured red-tiled houses exude an air of tranquillity where nothing much appears to move. The small island of Lazaretto, at the entrance to the harbour, was a place of quarantine from 1668 under the Venetians and English. After union with Greece, it was converted for use as a jail and eventually demolished by earthquakes.

There does not appear to have been a large settlement here before the sixteenth century but, according to ancient inscriptions, there may have been a temple to Artemis and some Roman tombs have been found. When pirate activity was quashed sometime during the six-

Odysseus on Ithaka and Kefalonia

Homer's *Odyssey* can arguably be described as the world's first novel complete with characters and a plot. Homer was actually a poet and a teller of myths and legends and his epic works, the *Iliad* and *Odyssey*, have become part of the literary heritage not just of Greece but of all nations of the world. The books represent two aspects of the Trojan War during the Mycenaean period which came to an abrupt end in 1100BC. The date of Homers work is not clearly known but thought to be around 700BC so he was relating legends which had been around for some 500 years. His works, a marriage of fact and fiction, have provided a battleground for scholars over centuries endeavouring to sort one from the other and identify fictional places with real locations.

The *Iliad* describes events in the east of the region, in what is now Turkey, but the *Odyssey* follows the travels of hero Odysseus, King of Ithaka, back home from the wars. Scholars have endeavoured to identify mythical places with locations in the Ionian islands which has generated many claims and counter claims from the islands themselves, and they are still arguing.

Apart from our hero Odysseus (Ulysses to the Romans), the story also has a 'goody' in the form of Athena, goddess of wisdom, who carefully guides Odysseus along his precarious voyage home, and a 'baddy', Poseidon, god of the sea. Poseidon is so enraged with Odysseus that he sows nothing but disaster and torment in his path back towards his homeland and faithful wife who spends all of her time fending off a plague of would-be suitors. Thanks to Poseidon's vindictiveness, it takes Odysseus ten years to get home from the wars although the nymph Kalypso took rather a fancy to Odysseus and kept him prisoner for seven years.

Ithaka naturally is full of references to Odysseus and Kefalonia too, mentioned as Sami by Homer, lays plenty of claims but these are mentioned in the appropriate places in the text.

Above: Frikes on Ithaka

Below: Kioni on Ithaka

teenth century, the old capital of Paliohora in the hills was moved down to Vathy. From then on, Ithaka developed a lucrative commercial maritime trade and began to prosper. Like Argostoli, it was a town of graceful Renaissance and neo-Classical style houses before the 1953 earthquake. Rebuilding after the earthquake mainly followed the old architectural style, a decree of 1978 further protecting it from unsightly development.

In the cathedral of 1580 is a particularly fine ikonostasis, carved by craftsmen from Metsovo on the mainland. The Archaeological Museum (open 8.30am-2.30pm; closed Mondays and holidays) houses a collection of artefacts found on the site of ancient Alalkomenes and elsewhere on the island. It lies one block back from the sign located on the harbour front. Continue following the road around the inlet to the ruined fortress of Loutsa, with cannons. This and another fortress, Kastro, opposite were built by the French in 1805 to defend the harbour entrance. The road ends at Loutsa by an organised swimming beach above which sits the fortress. Out to the south of Vathy are two more reputed Homeric locations, the Spring of Arethusa and the pig-pens of Odysseus' faithful swineherd Eumaeus.

The ruins of abandoned *Paliohora* lie close to the later village of Perahori in the hills behind Vathy. One time capital of the island, it nurtured a large population under the Venetians. Remains of its buildings indicate a defensive type of architecture and remnants of Byzantine frescos cling to the crumbling walls of roofless churches. When Vathy became the capital, the villagers gradually moved down to the coast and Perahori developed around the inhabitants who chose to remain in the hills.

Perahori, 300m (984ft) above sea level, lies in the hills above Vathy. This is the wine centre of Ithaka where a Wine Festival takes place at the end of August.

From Vathy, return along the main road north and keep ahead past the junction to Pisso Aetos. The road leads over the narrow Aetos isthmus and another Homeric site, that of Laertes field at Agros Laerti. After here the road splits, the lower route north to Stavros speeds traffic up the island via Lefki to Stavros. A road off right takes a more mountainous route to Stavros via the Kathara Monastery and village of Anogi.

Kathara Monastery stands at 600m (1,968ft) and is a good vantage point for views over the harbour. The monastery is dedicated to the Panagia Kathariotissa who is the island's protectress. It has been used since the late seventeenth century and a festival is held here annually on 8 September. There is thought to have been a temple to Artemis or Athena on the site and Lord Byron stayed here on route from Kefalonia to Messolongi, where he was to die a few months later. The road continues to Anogi through a landscape of rocks and shrubbery with views along the eastern coast of the island.

Anogi, meaning 'at the top of the world, sits at a height of 500m (1,640ft) and is one of the island's oldest villages. The twelfth-century Byzantine Church of the Assumption of the Virgin has an ikonostasis with fine fifteenth- and sixteenth-century ikons. Standing apart from the church is its seventeenth-century Venetian bell-tower. Anogi was once a fortified settlement the remains of which lie above the present day village. As with the villagers at Paliohora, the population of Anogi was much depleted once the pirate threat was removed as the people there relocated in Stavros and Kioni. On the outskirts of the village tower two huge rock formations of around 8m (26ft) in height. The villagers have named one Araklis (Heracles) which looks a little like a petrified cactus. From here, the road descends to Stavros.

Stavros is the main village of northern Ithaka but is less populated than it was when it was founded by the villagers of Anogi and Exogi during the sixteenth century. Unlike Vathy, which developed down at sea level, the populace of Stavros chose a site above the port of Polis. Stavros was an important cross-roads between the ports of Frikes and Polis becoming a convenient meeting point for traders from surrounding villages. A bust of the island's mythical king Odysseus in the main square is the only one of Homer's hero on the island. A narrow road off the

square leads in 1km (½ mile) down to the shingle beach and fishing harbour of Polis.

Polis is the suggested site of the ancient town of Jerusalem which was submerged by an earthquake in AD967 and Pilikata Hill, up to the right, yet another claimant to being the site of Odysseus' home the palace of Laertes. Finds from as early as the Neolithic era (2700BC) until Byzantine times have been found here including shards bearing Linear A script. Loizos cave, is located in the hillside to the right, and was probably a centre of worship during the Hellenistic period. Quite a few artefacts were excavated here, some dating back to prehistoric times and others from a later date which included amphorae, bronze tripods (800-700BC), used to hold vessels like amphorae, and figurines. A clay mask from around 200BC inscribed with a dedication to Odysseus, also found in the cave, points to local cult worship. These finds can be seen in the Pilikata Museum. After the end of the Hellenistic period the area remained unoccupied until the Venetians arrived.

Leave Stavros in the direction of Exogi. The Pilikata Museum is signposted up a narrow concrete road to the right half a kilometre from Stavros square (Open: 8.30am-3.00pm daily, closed Monday). The museum contains artefacts from the sites of Alalkomenes, Loizos Cave and the School of Homer.

Continue first to Exogi, meaning

Following Page: Ag Kyriakis Bay

Above: One of the Angonas wall murals

Below: The Assos peninsula

'outside the world', known in early times as *Stavronikion*. The name of the modern village of Stavros probably derives from this. Exogi clings to the mountainside with good views of the surrounding seas. At the highest point of the hill, from where there is a superb panorama of the Ionian islands and mainland Greece, is located the old monastery of Panagia Eleoussa. Platrithias is reached by returning through Exogi then turning left.

Platrithias (wide furrow) is the administrative centre for the clutch of villages at the top end of the island. Fertile soil, abundant water and ease of access to the ports of Frikes and Polis supported a population here from way back in early history until the Romans departed. Repopulation occurred about the same time as the founding of Vathy and Stavros, at the end of the sixteenth century. The eleventh-century Church of the Taxiarhi in the village was a monastery until the nineteenth century. More Homeric sites lie close to Platrithias with the Melanydrus Spring, whose therapeutic waters are said to have supplied the School of Homer and cured Homer's blindness, and 'Penelope's Baths' which are in fact Mycenaean tombs. A nearby section of ancient wall is said to be part of the school of Homer.

The fishing village of **Frikes**, possibly Homer's port of *Reithron*. Once inhabited by pirates, this picturesque bay is a small enclave shared by tourists and fishermen. Deserted mills dot the landscape

on the way round to the larger village of Kioni which spreads down the hillside to the attractive fishing harbour where yachts find anchorage. This was also once a pirate base which later blossomed then declined until tourism brought a revival of fortune.

CAR TOUR 1. THE NORTHERN PENINSULA

This excursion out of Argostoli enjoys the fine coastal and mountain scenery in the northern part of the island. Two of the island's most beautiful villages are included, Assos and Fiskardo, and there are a couple of irresistible beaches too so be sure to include a bathing costume and towel. Opportunities for refreshments are limited to the two villages mentioned otherwise pack a picnic. Allow a full day for the tour since both Assos and Fiskardo are especially beautiful and both require time to appreciate them. If only surfaced roads are to be used, the return route is the same as the outward route. Although the overall distance for the tour at 100km (62 miles) is not great, the twisting nature of the roads, and the scenery, operates against fast journeying. For those heading for a ferry, a straight run from Argostoli to Fiskardo takes around 1 ¼ hours.

Leave Argostoli by crossing Drapano bridge then heading north. Mountains dominate to the right while on the left there are views over

Argostoli Bay towards the Paliki peninsula. At Kardakata a road peels off left for Lixouri but it is straight ahead for Fiskardo. There are some ❋ extravagant wall murals to entertain near **Angonas** (Agonas) with the sight of a galleon in full sail or a young man helping an old lady up the stairs. These were painted by G. Lividas, a local folk artist. Also at Angonas is the road off down left to the inviting looking bay of Ag Kyriakis. Although the road starts surfaced it soon reverts to rough and difficult track and the reward for reaching the bay does not match the effort of getting there. A shingle beach awaits with a small harbour at one end and a taverna. By far the best approach by car is from the Lixouri road down through the village of Zola.

Once beyond Angonas the main road swings sharply inland following the contours of a gully. Watch here for the road off left down to the ⟋ spectacular **Myrtos Beach**. It is a surfaced road for most of the descent and there is just a short section of good track to contend with towards the end. Picturesque Myrtos beach offers a long stretch of white sand which slides away into an azure blue sea. The steep cliffs behind convert this bay into a sun trap but there is a bar on hand to help maintain liquid levels and there are sun beds and umbrellas for hire. Perhaps the best view of Myrtos beach is enjoyed from the main road when continuing on to Assos.

The headland jutting out into the sea seen from here is the location of Assos and there are fine views to absorb from the junction where the road leads down. Photographers 🦤 will want to pull off here but there are also good viewpoints along the descent road.

Assos clings and curls around the narrow neck of a peninsula and vies with Fiskardo for the title of most beautiful village on the island. There is an area for parking just over the narrow neck of the peninsula. Assos suffered severe damage from the earthquake of 1953 but was rebuilt in a pleasing style with funds provided by the French, which is why the square is now called Paris. Subsequent developments are also in sympathy with the character of the village. There are shaded tables outside the tavernas in the small harbour either for taking refreshments or enjoying a meal. It is easy to be absorbed by its relaxed atmosphere and allow time to melt away but there are things to do which include wandering up to the Venetian castle. 🏰

There is a choice of ways to reach the castle. A track leads up to the upper entrance which is fit for walking but in a bad state for motor vehicles, even for motorcycles, and there is a footpath to the lower entrance. The footpath starts to the right of the taverna at the foot of the headland. For a round trip walk up the track to the upper entrance, through the castle grounds to the lower entrance and return via the footpath. Built by the Venetians towards the end of the sixteenth century, this sturdy fortress protected 60 public buildings and 200 private houses from the rav-

Above: Assos village, one of the most attractive on the island

Below: Emblisi beach

ages of pirates. Even the harbour below was fortified. The extent of the fortifications on and around the headland, and much of them still stand, is best appreciated from a viewpoint on the Fiskardo road. It remained in the control of a Venetian governor appointed by the Great Council of the Republic until 1797 and afterwards it was used as a prison for a period. One of the first ruins to see when entering through the top gate is the catholic church of St Marcos built originally around 1604. There are other ruins still around including that of the governor's house but part of the inside is still used by the local farmers and the public are excluded. From the upper gate it is only necessary to follow the track as it winds down through the interior of the castle to reach the lower gate. From the lower gate a good footpath descends gently around the hillside and there is a point where it closes with the upward track and it is easy to cross to it, if preferred.

For Fiskardo, return up to the main road and head north once again. Watch out for a viewpoint over the headland at Assos to study the extent of the castle walls. Vasilikiades, the next village reached, is big enough to have a petrol station but do not count on it being open at weekends. From here the route becomes less mountainous and more rural, passing through a number of small villages. Just before Fiskardo is reached, there is a left turn down a surfaced road to **Emblisi Beach**, a small shingle beach lapped by sparklingly clear water. It is a totally natural beach without any sort of facilities at the moment.

Fiskardo is quickly reached from here and, unless heading for the ferry, it is necessary to park just outside and complete the journey on foot. For details of things to do and see in Fiskardo, see page 53.

CAR TOUR 2.
CAVES AND CRAGS

This excursion crosses to the eastern side of the island in search of adventure. The famous caves near Sami and two ancient sites are on the menu but the full itinerary includes ancient Krani, the Drogarati cave, Melissani cave, Sami, the beautiful beach of Anti Samos, ancient Sami and Ag Efimia before returning by a different route to Argostoli. It is a short tour in terms of distance, around 80km (50 miles), but there are more than enough highlights to fill the day and there is at least one alluring beach too difficult to ignore. A point on timing; Melissani is actually a collapsed cave containing a lake and is flooded with sunlight most effectively around midday. The best time to visit is between 11am and 1pm although it is still good outside these hours.

Leave Argostoli by crossing Drapano bridge over the harbour

Preceding page: The Assos headland

and follow signs to Sami. Almost immediately the road leads through a narrow gorge over a wooden bridge. Below here is the location of the small monastery of Ag Barbara although its bell tower can be seen on the rock above. In only around 3km (2 miles), look on the right for a blue sign for Krani which is located just before a road branches off left to Dilinata. Turn into the track and continue for around 2km (1¼ mile) until the cyclopean walls of ancient *Krani* are reached. It is an open site and there is no charge for entry. *Krani* was one of four ancient cities originating probably late in the Mycenaean era (1300-1100 BC). As the walls testify, it was very strongly fortified in typical Mycenaean style and some of the stout walls are built with huge polygonal stones. Walls of this type became dubbed cyclopean walls because subsequent generations were in awe of the enormous size of the stones used and believed that they must have been built by Cyclops, mythical one-eyed giants encountered by Odysseus in Homer's *Odyssey*. Said to stretch for 5km (3 miles), the walls enclose an area reaching down to the Koutavos Lagoon and considerable lengths of them have survived the earthquakes and still remain. Somewhere within these walls would have been an acropolis and its suggested location is to the east. The biggest threat to walls is from the ever encroaching trees and shrubs and the fight to keep them clear absorbs all the allowance for maintenance of this site.

Return back to the main road to continue towards Sami. A climb lies ahead before the Omala valley is reached which is the location of the Gerassimos monastery, visited in Car Tour 3. Stay on the main road to wind further up the flanks of the Ainos (Enos) range before reaching the fairly high level **Agrapidiaes Pass** around 550m altitude (1,805ft). The road which branches off right at this point to climb still higher into the mountains is explored in Car Tour 3. From here it is all downhill to Sami. Look for the left turn to Drogarati before reaching Sami.

Drogarati Cave is estimated to have developed over 150 million years although it was discovered only last century. As a commercial venture it has been open some 30 years. There is a charge to enter and exploration is on foot without a guide. Some 123 steps lead down the entrance shaft to a platform which gives the first view of the stalactites and stalagmites within the illuminated cavern. Further steps lead down from the platform to a walkway circling the lowest level of the cave. Angled lighting on the best formations brings out the textures and rich colours and helps to illuminate the path around. The acoustics are good in the cave and concerts are sometimes held there. It is also cool and damp and suitable footwear is advised since the wet rock and the steps can be slippery.

After leaving the caves, a side trip

Following page: Sami

Above: Ancient Krani, showing cyclopean Mycenaean walls

Below: The view down to Sami from ancient *Sami*

is possible to see the remains of the BC *Kastro of Sordhatos* built as a watchtower for Proni. Only walls remain to be seen but the road is surfaced all the way. Follow signs for Zervata and Digaleto then look on the right as the later village is entered.

Otherwise, it is just a short journey from the cave into Sami where parking should present no problems.

Sami is a major port and important holiday centre set in a large sweep of bay backed by mounds of green cloaked mountains. As other towns on the island, Sami was decimated by the 1953 earthquake and has since been rebuilt with spacious streets quite unlike the usual Greek town or village. The promenade is filled with shaded tables from the surrounding bars and tavernas and the wide streets house modern shops, including some of the best supermarkets on the island. Surprisingly pristine is the port area which sees daily ferries calling and departing for Ithaka and Patras with less frequent ferries from Italy. Shingle beaches lie either side of the promenade but for the best beach drive eastwards over the mountain to Anti Samos. It is a short 3km (2 miles) drive on a good road for most of the way, the last section is unsurfaced but sound, or a 45 minute walk with plenty of uphill work.

Anti Samos is one of those picturesque beaches which is impossible to resist. A crescent of white shingle snuggling into green cloaked hills shelves steeply into Homer's wine dark sea. It is a very beautiful beach and very natural but the facilities are limited. Drinks are available as well as sun beds and umbrellas but it seems destined to develop further.

The next destination in this tour is a diversion to locate the site of ancient Sami which involves some walking. It can easily be omitted if desired. On the return from Anti Samos, turn off left towards the top of the hill following a surfaced road signposted Moni Ag Agrilion. Stay ahead to join a track very shortly as the road swings left to the monastery and drive cautiously along for about 1km (½ mile) until the track becomes too rough to carry on further. Park here and continue on foot for around 30 minutes. The track leads around a valley and, once past a goat pen and hut on the right, the walls of the ancient city can be seen around the large hilltop on the right, Paliokastro, and the slightly lower hilltop, Ag Fanentes, next to it. Overgrown vegetation makes it impossible to approach the hilltop fortifications with any comfort but there are some ruins to inspect further on. The walls, built originally in the Mycenaean era, are believed to have contained twenty two entrances. Sami was perhaps the most important of the four ancient cities on the island and it remained inhabited at least until Roman times. As a city state it minted its own coins which testifies to its significance and size in that period. Homer mentions Sami as a participant in the Trojan wars and also mentions that a number of Penelope's suitors are Samians. History tells of how the inhabitants of Sami retired to their fortifications in 187BC and put up fierce resistance to the Romans withstanding battering rams and siege engines for a considerable time before they were eventually overcome.

Continue to follow the track enjoying views down over new Sami town until the ruins of a building Π and the small white church of Ag Nikolaos are reached. This is where the acropolis of Kyathis once stood and from here the ancient town spread down to the sea shore. Right at the bottom of this hill is the remains of a Roman villa where the bronze head was found which is now displayed in the museum in Argostoli. The old ruins here are of Ag Fanentes monastery and used in its construction are many stones of the ancient city. Nearby Ag Nikolaos is usually locked but there is an even older ruined church with frescos tucked away out of sight below the crown of the hill. To find it, take the steps down in front of the church and head left. A canopy protects the ruins but there is free access to inspect the collection of old frescos which decorate the apse and its surroundings.

This is the turning point of the walk and all that remains is to trek back to the car. Rejoin the road and turn back towards Sami. From Sami take the Ag Efimia road to head for the next port of call, the Melissani caves. Action starts on reaching the village of **Karavomylos** which is just 2km (1¼ mile) from Sami. On the right here, hidden behind Ag Io-

annis church bounded partly by trees and shrubs is the almost round lake of Karavomylos which is fed from the waters of Melissani cave. From here the water discharges into Sami bay through the Katovothres channel which starts over near Argostoli. A watermill once operated here but all that remains now is the large wheel and nearby is a lakeside taverna. Signs for Melissani cave are encountered a little further along the road.

Melissani Cave has a collapsed ☘ roof and contains a lake. It can only be explored by boat with the help of a guide. It is believed to take its name from melissa, the honey bee. Legend has it that this cave was dry in ancient times and in contact with the earth surfaces by narrow passages which bees used quite freely to swarm in the cave. Huge stalactites made of pure honeycomb filled the cave in those days but subsequent earthquakes have changed the structure of the cave and opened access to it. This is but one legend of many but it is certain that the cave has been around for some time since excavations in 1963 found some interesting ceramic objects. These included three oil lamps, a sculpture of a seated Pan and a magnificent large plate with a relief sculpture of five nymphs dancing around Pan to the music of his flute. This and the other objects found are displayed in the Archaeological museum in Argostoli. Some of these finds are believed to be from the fourth and third centuries BC.

The cave is entered by descending

Above: The route over to Anti Samos

Below: Anti Samos beach

Above: Ruins of Ag Fanentes monastery

Below: Karavomylos

down 20 steps to the landing stage where it is necessary to await one of the small boats. Each boat takes around fifteen people and is rowed by the boatman using two oars. A trip takes around ten minutes and the boatman rows across the lake, often through a pool of sunshine, to enter a narrower channel where oars are abandoned for a time in favour of a rope fastened along the cave wall. This section in the darker tunnel is short and then it is a reverse journey back to the landing stage. One or two rock features which form recognisable shapes, like a chicken head, are pointed out along the way. Deep and clear, the waters of the lake are fed from the Katovothres channel which arises near Argostoli and in turn feed the Karavomylos lake.

Continuing northwards, **Ag Efimia** is quickly reached. It is a small but attractive harbour town sitting in a deep bay and with hills close by. Shops and tavernas are on hand as well as a narrow shingle beach. Nothing seems to move very quickly to disturb the sleepy, rather intimate atmosphere. It might be hard to believe now but, before the earthquake of 1953, it was one of the island's more important centres of trade. Ferries run from the harbour here to Ithaka in high season. The town takes its name from the church of Ag Efimia near the harbour which celebrates its name day on 11 July . On this day the town really lets its hair down with processions, festivals and dancing; it is a great day to visit.

The route back from here crosses directly to the west coast and provides an opportunity to visit Myrtos beach, if not already visited in Car Tour 1. For Myrtos beach turn right on reaching the Argostoli-Fiskardo road and shortly left, otherwise turn left at the main road and continue back to Argostoli.

CAR TOUR 3.
SAINTS GEORGE AND GERASSIMOS

None of the car tours on the island are of any great distance and, at 75km (47 miles), nor is this. What it lacks in distance it makes up for in highlights. Included in the tour is the very summit, well almost, of the Ainos range, the monastery of Ag Gerassimos, a tasting at the nearby wine factory, St George's castle, remarkable Mycenaean tombs at Mazarakata, and, just in case a swim is in order, Avithos beach. Allow something over half a day for the tour which leaves plenty of time to enjoy the final call at Avithos beach.

Set off from Argostoli across Drapano bridge following signs to Sami. Ignore Ag Gerassimos monastery on the outward journey and save it for the return. Stay on the Sami road climbing up the side of the Ainos mountains to reach **Agrapidiaes Pass**. Turn off right here along the surfaced road which leads towards the mountain top. It climbs steadily, never dramatically, towards the summit of the mountain but the good road only lasts for 3km (2 miles) until the radar station is reached, beyond this it reverts to track. If it is time for refreshments, there is a kantina perched in the middle of a field near to the radar station. The onward 12km (7½ miles) track is in reasonably good condition and is maintained for the benefit of the television engineers who man the station near the summit of the mountain. However, winter rains can cause considerable erosion and there are always stretches which are less good and need to be taken with care. If the track is in bad condition, do not hesitate to turn back or park and walk. The summit area has been declared National Park largely to protect the Kefalonian fir, *Abies Cephalonica*, which is the dominant tree at these higher reaches (see feature page 30). The television station is reach-ed with steady driving but it is worth stopping here to walk the short distance on to the seated area from where there are superb views onto the east coast of the island. Return from here back to the monastery of Ag Gerassimos.

Ag Gerassimos is approached down a tree lined avenue which is interrupted only by a roundabout with a huge plane tree. Visitors are greeted at the entrance to the monastery's smaller church with an impressive bell tower which is fairly typical of the Ionian islands in architecture. Inside this highly ornate chapel, a silver casket standing near the ikonostasis contains the revered remains of the island's patron saint, Ag Gerassimos. He is celebrated on two special feast days, 16 August, the anniversary of his death, and 20 October, commemorating the date his bones were removed from his tomb. The Kefalonians are joined by pilgrims from all over Greece for the celebration of these special days. Inside the chapel, an iron ladder descends into the cave where Ag Gerassimos is said to have lived for a time on his arrival.

Ag Gerassimos is a fairly modern saint born in Trikala in Corinthia in 1507, son of a wealthy family. His ecclesiastical leanings were evident early in life when, in 1537, he went off to the Holy Land for 12 years and returned to take up Holy Orders. He settled in Zakynthos for a few years, living in a cave, before he came to Kefalonia and eventually settled in the Omala valley. Here, he took over an abandoned chapel to establish a nunnery and spent the remainder of his life tending the welfare of the villagers and their children. He died in 1579 and in the following years many miracles are claimed to have taken place. When his body was exhumed in 1581, it was found not to have decomposed and he was declared a saint.

The Omala plain is a fertile valley particularly good for growing grapes and it is here that Robola is made, one of the island's best known wines. The **Robola Producer's Co-operative**, open weekdays from 7am to 3pm, is tucked away behind the large church. Turn right on approaching the large church then left onto a track immediately beyond it. Here it is possible to look around the factory if wine making is in production or otherwise simply taste wines.

The Wines of Kefalonia

There are a number of wine producers on the island including the Robola Producer's Co-operative, Manzavino Wines and Calliga Wines. Of these only the Robola Producer's Co-operative encourages visitors to call in anytime to taste wines, Calliga sets aside Monday for wine tasting and Manzavino, located near Lixouri, is not open to casual visitors.

Robola is the name of a grape variety which is widely grown on the island and used by all the wine producers in the production of their white wines. A whole raft of varieties are used by manufacturers for their red wines which collectively are less good than the white.

Leading labels from the Robola Producer's Co-operative include Robola, a light, dry slightly fruity white, Brilliante, demi sec white and rosé which are both very easy to drink, Melambus a fragrant white and top of the range San Gerassimos which is made from specially selected robola grapes.

Calliga wines are perhaps the best known label outside Kefalonia. Again the robola grape is dominant in their white wines, particularly in Robola Calliga, a delicate white of superior quality. They probably make some of the better red wines on the island as their Cava Calliga which is matured in oak barrels. Calliga wines are usually easily recognised on supermarket shelves by the fancy bottles which are often used.

Manzavino is the trade mark of the Komitopoulos family who have been producing wines on Kefalonia for the past 300 years. Around ten labels are produced with a strong bias towards white wines and again the robola grape features strongly as in Robola de Kefalonia. Muscat, moscatela, tsaousi and goustolidi are the other grape varieties popularly grown on the island for white wines and all these are combined in Manzavino White Sec.

Apart from the branded wines, there is lots of local wine made on the island which is as good, often better, and certainly cheaper, than the commercial variety. Much of this wine is available in the tavernas so to try it ask for krasi dopio (local wine) or spitikokrasi (house wine). If the request is understood, a carafe or metal jug of wine should appear on the table, *yamas* (cheers!)

Above: The larger church at Ag Gerassimos

Below: The Robola wine factory

A road conveniently connects Ag Gerassimos with Travliata which is the next destination for St George's castle.

🏰 **St George's Castle** is firmly woven into the history of the island. This strategic location, on a peak at an altitude 320m (1,050ft), has probably attracted settlers from early times and, with the presence of Mycenaean tombs not too far away, it is tempting to believe that it has been occupied from this time. There are references to a castle there from the eleventh century but it firmly makes the history books in 1500 when a battleforce of Venetians supported by the Spanish fought hard to take it from the Turks. Improvements to the castle were made shortly afterwards, in 1504, when it took the form that is seen today. It became capital of the island and remained so until 1757 when the capital transferred to Argostoli.

Entrance is free and there is an extensive area to wander around inside. Most impressive are the mighty castle walls which still stand almost intact despite the earthquakes of the last couple of centuries but there are some interesting corners with ruined buildings to explore.

🏛 The Mycenaean tombs at **Mazarakata** are the next destination which are not signposted but should not be difficult to find with these instructions. From the castle head back down to the main Argostoli road, turn left into the centre of Travliata and take a right turn towards Metaxata. Turn right down the track immediately opposite the road signposted Pessada and ferries. A few hundred metres along is a fenced enclosure on the right by the track. A gateway allows entrance to this large Mycenaean cemetery which is remarkable for the variety of tombs it contains, some through shafts into the rocks.

For **Avithos Beach**, return back down the track and turn right towards Metaxata. Follow the road as it sweeps around right shortly and turn left towards Kourkoumelata and Calligata. Calligata is the home of Calliga wines but only Monday travellers can call in for a tasting session, it is closed to the public on other days. Roads become narrower around here but signs for the holiday complex Avithos Village also lead down to Avithos beach.

Avithos offers a picturesque beach of fine golden sand backed by cliffs. Access to the beach is down steps and facilities on hand include a beach bar and taverna, sun beds and umbrellas. There are some limited water sports in the form of pedaloes and boats. It is a great place to while away the rest of the day. For a different run back to Argostoli, head back through Metaxata to pick up the road via Lakithra which rides a ridge all the way back to Argostoli.

CAR TOUR 4.
SOUTHERN RESORTS

Tucked away in the south of the island are two of the island's main resorts, Poros and Skala. The road south skirts the lower contours of

Mount Ainos through the snake village of Markopoulo and on past the site of ancient Proni to Poros. This is a fairly large resort with the port area well away from the beaches. At present, only a scenic coastal track connects Poros directly with Skala but this is currently being upgraded. Lovers of sun, sand and sea will want to linger in Skala from where the road returns back up along the coast, calling at the more intimate beaches of Kato Katelios and Lourdas, to Argostoli. The tour covers a distance of around 100km (62½ miles) and there is ample opportunity to indulge in beach activities.

Follow the main route south out of Argostoli to Poros, which quickly leads past St George's castle to the foothills of Mount Ainos. Once past the right turn down to Lourdas at Vlachata, views open up along the coast from the elevated road. Keep ahead as the road branches right to Skala to soon reach the village of **Markopoulo**.

Every year around 15 August, the festival of Ag Maria, Markopoulo is infested with a small species of non-poisonous snake, thought to gather for breeding. This has been given a cloak of religious significance by villagers taking the snakes into the Church of the Panagia of Langouvarda. There, the snakes are placed on ikons and other religious artefacts and allowed to slither at will before disappearing as suddenly as they arrive. The story goes that they are nuns, who during a pirate raid, begged the Virgin to turn them into snakes. Their appearance is regarded as a sign of good luck and snake-draped locals happily pose for photographs.

Pass through the village of Pastra, from where a road/track connects down to Skala but this can be a little rough in places. Shortly after the main road swings inland, Ag Georgios is reached. A track off right leads round the hillside of Paleokastro and a right fork up, on a rougher track, which ends at the small Church of the Panagia. In this locality lay the ancient city and acropolis of *Proni*. Little remains of the site, but those prepared to scramble around the hillside might come across remnants of walls.

As the road bends right at **Tzanata**, history buffs have the chance to seek out a Mycenaean tholos tomb discovered on the outskirts of the village; to the right on leaving.

The road squeezes through a dramatic but short narrow gorge at the entrance to **Poros** and heads straight down to the sea front. A short walk to the left leads to the main sand/shingle beach, with an extensive array of watersports, although there is a clean pebble beach in the centre. Clear waters make ideal conditions for swimming and snorkelling and Poros is probably the most swinging resort on the island outside Lassi. Out of sight, beyond the headland to the right, is the port with ferry connections to Killini in the Pelopon-

Following page: St George's Castle

Above: Mount Ainos

Below: Poros village

nese. Phrygana covered **Mount Atros** provides a green backcloth for the pink oleander and yellow broom which splashes the streets with colour in early summer. A compact centre with plenty of shops and tavernas pander to tourist needs and there is no through traffic behind the main beach. High above the town on Mount Atros, reached by a stiff climb or in a four-wheel drive vehicle, sits the island's oldest monastery of Theotokos of Atros. If opting for the coastal route to Skala follow signs from the centre to the port over the headland. This is also thought to have been the port of ancient Proni and there are remains of walls closeby which suggests a fortified habitation of some kind.

Continue along the road beyond the port which winds up to become track. The track, which is being upgraded, follows closely along the pleasant coastline in gentle undulations for most of the way. Just before reaching Skala, the small chapel of Ag Georgios sits above the shore. This was the site of a sixth century BC temple to Apollo. A few broken Doric columns alongside the north wall of the chapel are immediately obvious but lying in a depression, a few steps further north, are the exposed temple foundations.

The present village of **Skala** was rebuilt at a lower level from the original after the 1953 earthquake. It exudes an altogether quieter ambience than Poros with a long, long deep sandy beach which is backed by shady pines at its centre. Watersports are also available. Skala itself is small scale and lies out of sight of the beach, up behind the pine wood. It makes an ideal family resort, especially for younger families. There are adequate facilities with a wide choice of reasonably priced restaurants/tavernas and shops along the one main village street. At the south part of the village are the remains of a Roman Villa. The foundations have been excavated to reveal a series of rooms with their mosaics intact. These have been left in situ with a protective roof covering and can be viewed even if the gate is locked.

Returning up the coast to Argostoli, call into the atmospheric fishing village of **Kato Katelios**. The village has a sand/shingle beach and pleasant tavernas and café/bars. It is slowly being turned into a small resort without, for the moment, losing its intimacy. Most of the new accommodation being built is scattered in a barren valley away from the village through which the onward route passes. Before reaching a left turn off to Mavrata there is a Mycenaean tholos tomb by the roadside, next to a small fenced-in house on the left.

Rejoin the Argostoli to Poros road and in seven kilometres, at Vlachata, turn left down to **Lourdas Beach**. The road winds down through Lourdata with its huge plane tree and shaded taverna to the coast. Although this is a popular beach there is little development apart from a few tavernas and some accommodation. An enticing turquoise sea fringed by silver sand and a dramatic mountain backdrop make this an ideal spot to end the day. A typically Greek fish taverna, Maga, juts out over the sand; perfect for an evening meal and watching the sunset.

EXCURSIONS FROM THE ISLAND

There are two very popular excursions to the mainland offered by tour operators; a day trip to Olympia and a two day trip to the capital, Athens. Both these can be done independently if desired. Regular service buses run from Kefalonia to Athens. A privately organised trip to Olympia would require a hire car and the economics are unfavourable unless the party size is at least four.

Olympia

Olympia is a small modern village which has grown in response to the influx of tourism. Hotels and tourist shops dominate but, in spite of the commercialism, it is a pleasant enough place for a short stay.

It is famed throughout the world as the birthplace of the panhellenic Olympic games which took place here every four years from 776BC to AD393. Unlike other great cultural centres of the period, Olympia was never a great city. It was a sanctuary built in the middle of a fertile plain by a spring at the foot of Mt Kronos, around 2000 BC, for the worship of Kronos, the father of Zeus, and the earth-goddess Rhea. The origin of the games is lost in a jumble of myths and legends. It may have started from a chariot race organised by King Oinomaos of Pisa who did not wish to lose his beautiful daughter Hippodameia by marriage. Suitors were invited to race their chariot against his to win his daughter but the penalty for losing was death. King Oinomaos was full of tricks to prevent being beaten but he was eventually outsmarted by Pelops. The linchpins in the King's chariot were replaced with some made of clay which held only long enough for the race to get underway. The King was killed in the accident and Pelops claimed his daughter. Alternatively, the origins may have been simpler. It is said that Heracles, son of the great Zeus who lived on Mt Olympos, marked out a sacred grove, the Altis, and introduced games in honour of his Olympian father.

In early Bronze Age religions, female deities were much in control and there is evidence to suggest that the early games involved women and remained that way until the worship of Zeus intruded. Myths and legends apart, the games were restarted in 776BC and the winners then and thereafter recorded. Pausanias claims that the prize first of all was for a footrace which was won in the first games by Koroibos of Elis. The race was over the distance of one stadion (192m). At the fourteenth Olympics, according to Pausanias, a two lap race was added and in the

Above: Pavos beach

Below: Roman villa, Skala

eighteenth the pentathlon (foot race, long jump, wrestling, javelin and discus) and wrestling. Eventually the games built up with the further introductions of boxing and equestrian events, including the very prestigious four horse chariot race and even races in armour. When the games became too large to be completed by dusk they were extended into the following days and they were truly panhellenic, open to all whose native tongue was Greek. So that all could attend, and there was virtually continuous warring in the various regions, a truce was strictly enforced and observed for the period of the games. It was clearly obeyed because the games continued with the utmost regularity. Male competitors only were allowed in the stadium and they, and their trainers, were obliged to demonstrate their sex by competing in the nude.

The prize for success at the games was nothing more than a garland of wild olive but it immortalised the victor and his family. Such was the prestige of the games that the wealth of the sanctuaries steadily accumulated and treasuries were built to accept the votive offerings from the various Greek states. The Romans were eventually accepted and admitted to the games which, after reaching new heights of professionalism, ended under the ban of Emperor Theodosius in AD393.

Excavation of the site by the Germans started in 1875 and lasted for a period of six years but there have been further excavations since, notably 1936-41 and 1952. All the finds are located in the excellent museum in the town. A consequence of the excavations was the eventual revival of the games; the first modern Olympiad being held in Athens in 1896.

The Site:
Within a few minutes walk from the centre of the village, the site lies in a silvan setting below Mt Kronos. In mid-April it takes on a haze of purple brilliance under the blossom of the Judas trees which flourish there.

Things To See:
The Palaistra: this square building from the third century BC, on the left after entering, was of uncertain purpose. It was either for wrestling and boxing or simply a meeting place. Some of its doric columns have been restored but originally there were colonnades on all four sides.

The Temple of Hera: both this temple and the Temple of Zeus lie within the Altis, a sacred area reserved for gods. It is a square area bounded on three sides by walls whose lines only can now be traced. The Doric Temple of Hera is the oldest temple on the site built around 600BC on foundations which are even earlier. The earlier wooden columns were replaced by stone in various styles. Four columns have been restored and there are several partial columns in place.

Preceding page: Brightly woven slippers, Fiskardo

The Temple of Zeus: built by Libon of Elis and completed around 457BC, this Doric style temple was one of the largest in Greece. In spite of the sixth-century earthquake, the foundations and many of the column bases and capitals survived allowing some restoration. Similarities with the Parthenon in Athens suggest that the same architect, Pheidias, may have been involved with the design.

Nymphaion fountain: this semicircular fountain, close to the Temple of Hera, was built by the Athenian Herodes Atticus around AD160.

Treasuries: lying adjacent to the fountain towards the stadium and built on a terrace overlooking the Altis, the treasuries were in effect small temples built by various cities to house their votive offerings.

The Stadium: in spite of all that is fine on the site, this is the biggest attraction to many visitors. The stadium as it is presently seen is the result of excavations and restoration by the German Archaeological Society in 1961-2 to its fourth-century form. There was no seating, only earth embankments to seat some forty thousand spectators and the starting and finishing lines can still be seen.

The **Archaeological Museum** is housed in a modern building at the far end of the car park which is opposite the archaeological site. A prior visit to this excellent museum is worthwhile if only to see the scale model of the site which helps with locating the various buildings and visualising Olympia as it was in a late stage of its development. The excavations unearthed a treasure of finds from helmets and shields through to votive offerings, most of which are now housed in chronological order in the museum. Amongst many fine exhibits, one highlight is the sculptures from the Temple of Zeus in the central hall. The sculpture from the east pediment is thought to commemorate the chariot race between King Oinomaos and Pelops.

A history of the Olympic games in memorabilia is contained in the Museum of Olympic Games located to the rear of the village on the west side.

Athens

The lure of Athens lies in a romantic vision of an age long since past. A pastoral vision of graceful architecture, greenery and tumbling streams. The present day reality is a high density sprawl. A huge ugly concrete monster with an insatiable appetite intent on devouring all in its path. Even the restraining hills seem in danger of being swamped. Add to this noise, dirt and pollution and one may wonder why anyone still bothers to go at all but go they do. In the middle of this concrete jungle still lie the remains of Athens' ancient glory where it is still possible to escape into the past.

Byron's view of Athens in 1809 was succinctly expressed in this apt couplet and there has been no improvement since.

Above: Olympia

Below: Topless bathing is commonplace on beaches, but nudity is illegal

> Shrine of the mighty! Can it be
> That this is all remains of thee?

The removal of the capital of newly liberated Greece from Nafplio to Athens in 1834 provided an ideal opportunity for improvement. There followed a period of planned building construction in neo-classical style but dreams of repeating Perikles achievement were abruptly ended in 1922 as a result of the Greek-Turkish war in Asia Minor. The ethnic population exchange which ensued witnessed an influx of political refugees. Unable to keep pace with housing demands, shanty towns mushroomed in outlying areas. The problem was further aggravated by World War II followed by civil war and a subsequent massive population movement from rural areas into the city.

Athens lies in the Attica basin surrounded by the mountains of Parnes (1,413m/4,637ft), Pendeli (1,107m/3,633), Hymettus (1,026m/ 3,367ft) and Egaleo (468m/1,536ft). Its current problems are compounded by its geographical position and a population which has almost quadrupled to around four million people in the past forty years; over a third of the population of Greece. The attendant pollution from industry and cars is trapped by the surrounding ring of mountains and, in summer, the nefos lies like a yellow blanket over the city.

The major sites and points of interest in Athens are confined to a relatively small area within the city centre and a surprising amount can be achieved in the course of one day. Six tours are offered here to cover the best of Athens, from archaeological site to shopping expeditions. It should be possible to choose a balanced programme to cover most interests. Perhaps the first port of call should be the Greek National Tourist Office in Syndagma square to collect a street plan of the capital.

TOUR 1. ANCIENT ATHENS: THE ACROPOLIS AND THE AGORA

A visit to Athens is synonymous with a visit to the Acropolis. As long ago as 7,000BC Stone Age man was attracted to the hill and built one of the earliest settlements in Greece on its slopes. During the Mycenaean era it was peopled by successive priest-kings and their retainers who lived in a palace on the site. The remains of cyclopean walls stem from this time. From 1100BC there followed a period of transformation which saw the decline of the palace culture of the Minoan-Mycenaean world. This dark age, about which little is known, lasted for several hundred years and ended with the emergence of the polis or Greek city-state and the beginnings of democracy. Temples to the gods of the polis replaced the palace and other secular buildings on the Acropolis but these were destroyed by the Persians in 480BC.

Preceding page: An Evzone guarding the tomb of the unknown warrior

Athens' brief period of glory or Golden Age lasted for 32 years from 461BC during the time Perikles was head of state. Using the Delian League funds, which had been transferred by the Athenians from Delos to the Acropolis, Perikles embarked on an ambitious building plan. His construction programme was executed in an amazingly short span of time, the Parthenon itself taking only ten years to complete. After Perikles' death Athens never regained the prosperity and growth it had enjoyed under his rule falling prey to the various uses and misuses of successive conquerors.

The most pleasant way to approach the Acropolis is through Plaka, from Syndagma via Nikis, Nikodimou, Flessa and up left off Lissiou, thus avoiding the busy road which runs beneath its southern flank. A paved path, just below the Acropolis, passes an entrance to the Agora and the Areopagus, visited later in the tour, before joining the main route up to the Acropolis. Facilities close to the main entrance include a bank, post office, refreshments, cloakroom/left luggage (in season) and WCs. To avoid the sizzling heat in summer make an early start.

Beware of the treacherous highly polished marble underfoot!

The Sacred Way: This ancient route (20km/12miles) ran between the Sanctuary of Eleusis (Elefsina) passing through the ceremonial Sacred Gate, adjacent to the Dipylon Gate, and through the Agora before rising up to the Propylaia.

The Beule Gate: A Roman addition built in AD third century and the entrance to the Acropolis site.

The Propylaia: Is the name given to the group of buildings which make up the original entrance complex. The Propylon being the actual entrance built, in this case, to resemble a temple.

The Temple of Athena Nike: An exquisite temple situated high up to the right of the Propylaia.

The Erechtheion: The Temple to Athena and Poseidon built on the most sacred part of the Acropolis. On this site the two gods were believed to have held their contest to decide who ruled Athens. Its appeal today is sight of the six graceful Karyatides (copies) and the deceptive ease with which they support the porch. The original Karyatides have been removed, one by Lord Elgin and the remainder into a protective atmosphere within the Acropolis Museum.

The Acropolis Museum: Unob- trusively built on lower ground to the east of the Parthenon. Here, in addition to various pottery finds and statues, are the original Karyatides, fragments of friezes, the Almond-Eyed Kore, the Kritios Boy, the Calf-Bearer and a sculpture of the graceful, winged figure of Athena Nike untying her sandal.

The Parthenon: The Temple of Athena Parthenos (Temple of the Virgin Athena) stands proudly aloof from crass modernity, despite its tumultuous history, and continues to epitomise all that was ancient Greece. Rampant erosion is the

Above: Karyatides supporting the porch of the Erechtheion on the Acropolis

Below: The Parthenon on the Acropolis

present enemy and constantly threatens to overwhelm ongoing restoration work.

The Theatre of Dionysos: The most famous theatre of the Greek world nestling into the south-east side of the hill beneath the Acropolis. Most of the present day remains are Roman.

The Asklepion: A healing sanctuary built close to the Theatre of Dionysos. A natural location considering the close relationship between drama and healing.

The Stoa of Eumenes: Costructed in the second century BC as a shelter and promenade along a section of the peripatos close to the Theatre of Dionysos. It was later connected to the Odeon of Herod Atti-cus by the Romans.

Odeon of Herod Atticus: Built into the south-west slope of the hill in AD second century and restored for present day use. The Odeon is normally closed, except for performances, and the best view of it can be had from the Acropolis.

The Peripatos: The ancient road around the lower Acropolis.

Returning now towards the Agora:

The Areopagus (Hill of Ares): A small hill across a saddle to the north-west of the Acropolis hill. It was on this site the Council of Areopagus met to rule on matters of justice and in AD 51 Saint Paul preached the new gospel. Provides an excellent vantage point for a bird's eye view of the Agora.

The Agora: Once the hub of ancient Athenian life, now a welcome retreat. Amongst the ancient foundations stand the AD tenth-century Church of the Holy Apostles and the Stoa of Attalos now rebuilt and housing the museum. On a rise in the north-west corner of the Agora is the excellently preserved Thesion or Temple of Hephaistos. From the temple there is a good view over the Agora to the Acropolis.

TOUR 2. HILL OF THE MUSES: FILOPAPPOU HILL AND THE PNYX

Filopappou Hill, with its huge monument, and the Hill of the Pnyx are usually only accorded a passing glance by most people as they pause in their scramble around the Acropolis. Their wooded slopes though, criss-crossed with footpaths, provide a welcome retreat from the city heat. The reward for a walk up to the monument is a clear view of the Acropolis and over the city.

Follow the same route through Plaka as for Tour 1 but continue on the main path down to Dion. Areopagitou road. Cross the road and head right towards the roundabout from where a cobbled road leads up onto Filopappou Hill and over to the Filopappou Theatre.

Filopappou Hill: Known also as the Hill of the Muses provides extensive walkways amongst its tree clad slopes. Follow a path off left of the

Preceding page: The Acropolis

cobbled road to take you up to the huge monument dedicated to a Roman senator and consul, Filopappos. On the way up there are pleasant areas with old marble seats where you can rest and drink in the views over Athens. Heading back down towards the Pnyx, pass the Prison of Socrates and the Byzantine church of Ag. Demetrios with its original frescos.

Pnyx Hill: Questions relating to public policy were debated by the Athenian Assembly on this hill. The area is now used for a Sound and Light show in summer. On the south-west side of the hill is a large picnic area with tables and drinking water fountains. Extensive views stretch beyond Piraeus to the sea.

Hill of the Nymphs: The site of the Observatory and gardens. Only occasionally open to the public.

TOUR 3. CITY PANORAMA: KOLONAKI SQUARE-DEXAMENI SQUARE-LIKAVITOS HILL

The narrow streets off sophisticated Kolonaki Square teem with boutiques for the fashion conscious and, without the constant roar of traffic, drinking coffee and people-watching could be a pleasant pastime at one of the pavement cafés in the square itself. On the plus side, a rarely encountered feature are public toilets kept in pristine condition. The 15 minutes walk to Likavitos funicular station starts from this square and takes you up through Dexameni Square with its quieter ambience. Likavitos Hill (277m/909ft), the ultimate destination, is the highest point in Athens and the place to go for a complete panoramic view over the city and beyond. It is particularly renowned for viewing spectacular sunsets. Start your wander up pedestrianised Skoufa and on the corner of Iraklitou, where you turn right, is Everest one of the best take-away food shops in the area.

Head up into leafy Dexameni Square with its outdoor café tables and the site of a reservoir begun by the Emperor Hadrian. Continue along Dinokratous as far as Ploutarchou. A left turn here will take you directly up to the funicular station for the 2 minutes ascent of Likavitos. One of the many footpaths and the most direct (15 minutes) starts 2 minutes along to the west of the station. The winding path passes a café/bar around halfway up and emerges by the small white chapel dedicated to St George, on the very top above the restaurant. An alternative path down from the lower terrace leads past the Likavitos Theatre used for Greek dance performances in summer.

TOUR 4. THE NATIONAL ARCHAEOLOGICAL MUSEUM

Situated north of Omonia Square in Patission, this vast museum demands at least a good half-day of

Above: The Tower of the Winds

Below: Flea market souvenirs in Monastraki

Above: Organ grinder in the Plaka area

your time. Time, and lots of it, is required to fully appreciate the sheer quality of artistry in such volume. To reap the benefit of a visit you do need a guide or a detailed guide book as the wonderful exhibits are unimaginatively displayed and labelling is almost non existent. Despite these drawbacks, the displays are housed in defined areas of the museum. By far the biggest draw is the Mycenaean Hall (Room 4) housing Schliemann's gold finds from Mycenae including what he wrongly believed to be the gold death mask of Agamemnon. How long they will remain on display in Athens is a moot point as they are scheduled to be rehoused in an on-site museum at Mycenae. Amongst the Classical Art collection can be found the bronze fifth-century BC Statue of Poseidon (Room 15) and the Little Jockey (Room 21) both reclaimed from the sea off Evia. Lifelike sculptures of the Youth of Antikythera (Room 28) and the heads of a Boxer, Philosopher and Man from Delos with his superbly captured poignant expression (Room 30). A naked Aphrodite (Room 31) excites a great deal of attention but the many sensitively sculpted Stelai provide an insight into the everyday life of the people of the time. Also not to be missed are the fantastic Thira frescos, upstairs in Room 48, restored to their original position on the walls to show how they would have looked about 3,450 years ago. Add to this rooms full of pottery and smaller finds plus an extensive Numismatic Collection, in a separate museum, on the first floor and you will almost certainly be left with the feeling that you have not been able to give full justice to your visit. The Numismatic Museum can be entered from outside, from Tositsa, or from inside the Archaeological Museum on payment of a separate entrance fee.

TOUR 5. OLD ATHENS. PLAKA-TOWER OF THE WINDS-FLEA MARKET

A stroll round Plaka's narrow streets conjures up a romantic image of an age past and is particularly atmospheric in the evening. Monastiraki on the other hand is a noisier more bustling quarter during the day and the location of the Flea Market.

Start out from Syndagma Square (Platia Syntagmatos) down Mitropoleos, which leads past the Cathedral to Monastiraki, and turn left up Nikis to locate the souvenir shopping streets of Kidathineon and Adrianou.

Plaka, the oldest residential area in Athens on the lower northern slope of the Acropolis Hill, is a pleasure to explore. Its many narrow streets and alleyways hiding a few quiet backwaters especially in Anafiotika where mid-nineteenth century construction workers from the island of Anafi built their homes. Busy, pedestrianised Kidathineon and Adrianou are lined with numerous souvenir shops their wares spilling out onto the streets in a kaleidoscope of colour. Adrianou stretches from the Thesion by the Ancient Agora almost to Hadrian's Arch passing the metro station at Monastiraki and the Monument of Lysicrates which carried the bronze tripod he won in a drama contest. Squeezed into an area off Adrianou at its junction with Eolou, below the Acropolis, is the Roman Agora and the first-century BC Tower of the Winds, a water clock, compass, weather vane and sundial. Tavernas and cafés abound for mellow evenings spent eating and drinking in one of Plaka's leafy squares to the sound of a bouzouki or, for more robust Greek evenings, in a night club environment.

Merging into Plaka, Monastiraki

and its bazaar-like atmosphere is where to head for a taste of more authentic Greek life, especially to the west of Monastiraki square. The Flea Market starts down Pandrossou which runs from the bottom corner of the cathedral square on Mitropoleos. Across Monastiraki Square ✳ the Flea Market fills narrow Ifestou with an amazing array of goods for sale and exudes a more homespun air. The square itself has been the core of a market area since Turkish times. A past which is still very much alive today in the cacophony of sound from barrel-organ players to the many street vendors touting lottery tickets, nuts, fruit, drinks and various snack foods. Every Sunday the flea market cascades into the surrounding streets attracting throngs of Athenians in search of a bargain.

TOUR 6. SHOPPING

Compared with most other major cities Athens' shopping centre is contained within a relatively small area. Situated on the north side and adjacent to the city's ancient quarter, it is easily accessible to most tourist hotels. Also to be found in the same area are a clutch of Byzantine churches all fighting for survival amidst the concrete and car exhaust fumes. The suggested route provides a good overview but, with more time to spare, further exploration of narrow streets like Leka and Praxitelous are worthwhile.

Syndagma Square makes a good starting point for a shopping expedition. Head along Mitropoleos en route to Athens Cathedral (Metropolis) which dwarfs its much more interesting predecessor the twelfth-century AD church of Ag Eleftherios. Leave the Cathedral Square along Evangelistrias to reach the clothing shops and Byzantine church of Kapnikarea, now a traffic island in the middle of the road, on Ermou. Escape the traffic by turning up towards Omonia into a pedestrianised section of Eolou to pass the colourful flower market alongside the church of Ag Irini. Spare time also to pause and look back for the best view of the Tower of the Winds against the backdrop of the Acropolis hill before turning left towards Athinas on reaching Evripidou. A right turn into Athinas and the clamour of human activity competes with the roar of traffic around the Meat and Fish Market on the right and the Fruit and Vegetable Market on the left.

Hurtling traffic, squealing tyres and scurrying crowds epitomise Omonia Square, the heart of the student quarter. Passageways and arcades lined with shops and fast-food outlets run off the square and provide a welcome diversion from the constant noise and congestion. The larger department stores are also situated in the vicinity.

Continue out to the east of Omonia Square crossing Ermou then back down El. Venizelou, better known as Panepistimiou, in the direction of Syndagma. The fashionable shopping area around Kolonaki Square completes the circuit.

FACTS FOR VISITORS

ACCOMMODATION

Hotels

These are classified by the GNTO into De Luxe, AA and A class which are subject to a minimum price structure only. Bars, restaurants and swimming pools are the facilities that you expect to find but, on a cautionary note, the class in itself isn't a guarantee of the standard of service. Kefalonia has no luxury class hotels and only a handful of A class.

In addition there are B, C and D classes for which maximum and minimum room rates are fixed by the GNTO.These hotels are obliged to display their category and price behind the door of each room. There is no C in the Greek alphabet so this class is represented by the gamma sign (Γ). Extra charges described as taxes or service may be added to the final rate and you need to check each time. Note that the charge is normally a room charge, not a charge per person and may or may not include breakfast. Room charges are seasonal with low, mid and high season rates. It is possible to bargain, especially for a stay of three days or more, but you are most likely to succeed when business is slack out of high season. Generally the C class hotels have rooms with bathrooms as do many of the D class but here it is not obligatory. Many of these hotels are often family run and offer a good level of cleanliness and comfort. The lower grade hotels may not have bar or restaurant facilities, except for breakfast.

Villas and Apartments

The vast bulk of the accommodation on Kefalonia falls into this category. Many, but not all, are in the hands of letting agencies who place them with tour operators. In early season a lot of apartments stand empty and, and even though they may be contracted out, it is still possible to make private arrangements on the spot, sometimes at very attractive rates. Otherwise, it is a question of driving around looking for Rooms to Let signs and making enquiries either locally or through the GNTO or the Tourist Police.

There is not an abundance of hotels on the island and the following is a selection taken from various categories:

Ag Efimia

(Telephone code 0674)

Hotel Pylaros (C), 10 rooms. ☎ 61210

Logara (Furnished apartments) (C), 23 rooms. ☎ 61202

Argostoli

(Telephone code 0671)

Hotel Aenos (C), 40 rooms. ☎ 28013

Hotel Argostoli (C), 21 rooms. ☎ 28358

Hotel Cephalonia Star (C), 38 rooms. ☎ 23180-3

Hotel Galaxias (C), 33 rooms. ☎ 24096

Hotel Phocas (C), 44 rooms. ☎ 28100

Vivian Apartments, 9 excellent rooms and apartments. ☎ 23396

Lassi

(Telephone code 0671)

Hotel Mediterranee (A), 227 rooms. ☎ 28761-3

White Rocks (A), hotel and bungalows, 163 rooms. ☎ 28332-4

Hotel Irilena (C), 22 rooms. ☎ 23172

Hotel Lassi (C), 32 rooms. ☎ 23126

Hotel Lorenzo (C) 45 rooms. ☎ 28783

Lixouri

(Telephone code 0671)

Kefalonia Palace (A), located at Xi, 36 rooms. ☎ 91111 Fax 92638

Hotel Ionian Sea (B), 24 rooms. ☎ 92280

Il Giardino (Furnished Apartments) (B), 7 rooms. ☎ 92505

Hotel Summery (C), 56 rooms. ☎ 91771

Poros

(Telephone code 0674)

Belvedere (Furnished Apartments) (B), 26 rooms. ☎ 72493-4

Hotel Kefalos (C), 29 rooms. ☎ 72139

Sami

(Telephone code 0674)

Hotel Perikles (B), 71 rooms. ☎ 22780-6 Fax 22787

Hotel Sami Beach (B), 44 rooms. ☎ 22824

Hotel Ionian (C), 16 rooms. ☎ 22035

Skala

(Telephone code 0671)

Hotel Skala (C), 8 rooms. ☎ 83202

Tara Beach (Bungalows) (C), 45 rooms. ☎ 83250

Ithaka

(Telephone code 0674)

Hotel Mendor (B) 36 rooms. ☎ 32433

Odysseus (Pension) (B) Vathy, 10 rooms. ☎ 32381

Hotel Nostos (C) Frikies, 30 rooms ☎ 31644

Camping

Camping in areas other than on official camping grounds is not permitted in any part of the island. It is something which the Greek authorities tend to get uptight about, especially in popular tourist regions.

There are two camp sites, Argostoli Beach (☎ 0671 23487) Karavomylos Beach, Sami (☎ 0764 22480).

CAR HIRE

Car hire is popular and many visitors take a car for three or four days which is generally enough to see the various parts of the islands. A current driving licence is required for EU nationals and others should have an International Driving Permit. The hirer must be over 21 for a car and 25 for a jeep or a minibus. If there is any intention to take the car on ferries, it is not a problem but it must be sanctioned by the hire company.

Kefalonia is expensive for car hire and a better deal can be arranged by booking and paying in advance of departure, not necessarily through a tour company but through companies like Transhire (☎ 071 978 1922 and Fax 071 978 1797) which offer good rates and include full insurance and unlimited mileage. These companies operate through an agent on the island and offer rates significantly lower than those available from the agent on the spot.

There is no shortage of car hire companies on the island but advertised car hire rates are very often the basic rates exclusive of insurance, mileage and tax. Third party insurance is compulsory under Greek law and this cost will be added to the hire charge. An additional optional insurance is collision damage waiver (CDW) and it is imperative to take it. This cannot be stressed too strong-ly. Should you be unfortunate enough to be involved in an accident without CDW insurance and the costs cannot be recovered from a third party then the consequences can be frightening. At best you may be faced with a huge repair bill, at worst you could end up in jail until it is fully paid. On short one or two day hires mileage is limited to 100km/day and a rate applies for excess kilometres. On top of all this is VAT at 18 per cent.

Tyres and damage to the underside of the car are mostly excluded from the insurance cover. Take time when you are accepting the car to inspect the tyres and, if not fully satisfied, do not accept the vehicle. It is worth a moment too to check that lights and indicators are fully operational. Greek law demands that a car must also carry a fire extinguisher, first aid kit and a warning triangle.

Motorcycles

Above comments on insurance apply also to hiring a motorcycle or moped. There is a problem over crash helmets too. The law says very clearly that these must be worn but the chances that you will be able to hire them along with the bike are slim. Do ask since a number of agencies have helmets but only produce them if they think that they are about to lose some business. It is an unhappy situation which only compounds the personal dangers to motorcyclists in a country which has a very high accident rate. Make sure before you depart that the lights work. If you intend to hire a motorcycle, it is worth checking the fine print in the medical section of the holiday insurance taken out in your home country. Such is the concern over motorcycle accidents that some companies are specifically excluding injuries arising this way.

See also Driving on Kefalonia.

CHANGING MONEY

Banks are in extremely short supply outside Kefalonia town but there are plenty of Exchange Bureaux around to compensate. This is fine for visitors exchanging bank notes or Travellers Cheques but less convenient for holders of Eurocheques. For the latter the Bureaux charge a commission, usually 2 per cent, on top of the commission charged by the bank. Normally, the Bureaux are open for much longer hours than the bank, sometimes extending well into the evening. Hotels also offer exchange facilities but generally their rates are less favourable.

For those travelling into Kefalonia town to use the banks then the opening hours are as follows: Monday to Thursday 8am–2pm, Friday 8am–1.30pm. Post Offices sometimes offer exchange facilities and they are open on weekdays from 7.30am–2pm, closed on Saturday and Sunday.

CONSULATES

There are no consuls on the island but the Tourist Police are empowered to issue a temporary exit in the event of a lost or stolen passport. If there is sufficient time, they will fax the Embassy in Athens to obtain a temporary passport.

Nearest foreign Embassies and Consulates are:

Australia
37 D Soutsou Street & An Tsocha
115 21 Athens
☎ 6447303

Consular Help

Consular help is on hand in times of emergency but this is largely in an advisory capacity. The following comments are offered in terms of guide lines only and do not fully define the powers of the office. The Consul can:

Help with problems over a lost passport and issue an emergency one if necessary.

Help with problems over lost money or tickets but only by contacting relatives or friends at your request to ask them to provide the finance needed.

Advise on the details of transferring funds.

Encash a cheque supported by a valid banker's card but only in an emergency and as a last resort when there are no other options.

Make a loan to cover repatriation expenses when this is the absolute last resort.

Arrange for next of kin to be informed following an accident or death and advise on procedures.

Act for nationals arrested or imprisoned to inform relatives

Give guidance on organisations experienced in tracing missing people

Provide a list of local interpreters, English speaking doctors and solicitors .

They do not involve themselves in finding work or obtaining work permits. Neither will they investigate a crime, give legal advice, instigate legal procedures on your behalf or attempt to interfere with the Greek legal procedures. Nationals in hospital or imprisoned can only expect the same treatment as the Greeks and the Consul has no power to gain better conditions.

Canada
4 I. Genadou Street
115 21 Athens
☎ 7239511-9

New Zealand
15 -17 Toscha Street
115 12 Athens
☎ 6410311-5

USA
Embassy-Consulate
91 Vass. Sophias Avenue
115 21 Athens
☎ 721951-9

UK
Consul
Votsi 2
Patras
☎ 061 276403

CRIME AND THEFT

On an island like Kefalonia, crime and theft levels are low and incidences of violence rare. There is no need to feel threatened in any way, even throughout the evening, but it is sensible to be cautious late at night, especially women on their own.

Many hotels have safety deposit boxes available for guests at a small charge. Otherwise, keep valuables out of sight. This is particularly true if you have a car. Cameras, personal stereos and the like are best carried with you but if you need to leave them in the car make sure they are locked in the boot.

If you are unfortunate enough to suffer a loss through theft or carelessness then report it to the Tourist Police. There is a form to complete if an insurance claim is contemplated.

If your loss includes a passport then you will need to contact the Tourist Police (see Consulates).

CURRENCY AND CREDIT CARDS

The local currency is the drachma which is indicated by drx or simply Dx (ΔP) before the number. Drachma notes commonly in circulation include 10,000, 5,000, 1,000 and 500 with just a few 100 and 50 drachma notes still around and coins of 100, 50, 20, 10 and 5 drachma value. The 100 and 50 drachma notes are steadily being replaced by coins but are still legal tender. The new 100, 50 and 20 drachma coins are all gold coloured and differ only in size. The 100 and 50 drachma coins in particular are easy to confuse. Some of the 20 drachma coins are still silver as are those of lesser value. Avoid bringing home coins and low value notes since most banks refuse to change them.

Travellers cheques, Eurocheques and hard currencies are freely accepted at banks, Post Offices and Exchange Bureaux. Credit cards and charge cards are also widely accepted in hotels, shops and restaurants especially in Argostoli.

Although it is possible to get a

Preceding page: Ag Efimia

cash advance on a credit card, there still seems to be some suspicion of this transaction. Only certain banks will co-operate and the best ones to try are the National Bank of Greece and the Commercial Bank. There is a minimum size of transaction, around 15,000 drachmas.

Always take your passport when changing money. Even though the production of a passport may not be a necessary requirement, the Greeks rely on them as a means of identification. You may even be asked for it when purchasing an internal flight ticket. The cost of changing money in terms of commission does vary and it pays to check; normally the cheapest place is at a bank and the worst place is the hotel reception.

DRIVING ON KEFALONIA

Driving on Kefalonia is on the right hand side of the road and overtaking on the left. In the event of an accident where the driver was proven to be on the wrong side of the road, the insurance is invalidated. Unless there are signs indicating otherwise, the speed limits are as follows: built-up areas 50kph (31mph), outside built-up areas 80kph (50mph). Seat belts must be worn by law. The use of main beam headlights in towns and cities is forbidden as is the carrying of petrol in cans.

Unleaded petrol *(amolivthi venzini)* is freely available on Kefalonia but not always in the country areas. The grades of petrol *(venzini)* nor-

mally on offer are unleaded, Super-unleaded and Super at 96/98 octane. Diesel is also widely available and, like petrol, is sold by the litre.

Parking in Argostoli is not too much of a problem at the north end of the town but can be difficult in the central areas at busy times. It pays to observe street parking restrictions, often ignored by the Greeks but illegal parking can result in a ticket and a hefty fine. The ticket indicates the amount of the fine and where and when to pay it. The police are not empowered to collect on the spot fines.

With one of the worst accident rates in Europe, driving in Greece demands a cautious attitude from the onset. The discipline shown by the majority of drivers in western European countries, which brings order to traffic flow, is often missing from Greek drivers but Kefalonian drivers are a little more orderly. Drive with your own safety in mind. Another major hazard is the state of the roads. Pot holes are always a danger and can be encountered unexpectedly even on well surfaced roads. A line of rocks on the road guiding you towards the centre is the usual warning of edge subsidence and there will often be no other warning signs. Minor roads, which are well surfaced, may suddenly become unmetalled. Road works may have no hazard warning signs or irregular ones such as a pile of earth or a milk crate with a small flag.

Here is a quick check on some of

Above: The lake at Karavomylos

Below: The beach at Poros

the hazards frequently encountered: uncertain rights of way, limited road markings, narrow roads, sharp edges, potholes, ill placed road signs, Greek drivers driving the wrong way through a one way system, sheep, goats and donkeys, motorcyclists without lights, and pedestrians where there are no footpaths.

Information on all aspects of motoring can be obtained from the Automobile Association and Touring Club of Greece, ELPA, Athens Tower, 2-4, Messogion Street, 15 27 Athens. ☎ 7791 615 to 629 and 7797 402 to 405

Road signs

Fortunately, international road signs are used throughout the island but there may be occasions when you encounter temporary signs written in Greek. Here are a few examples:

ΑΛΤ – Stop
ΕΛΑΤΤΩΣΑΤΕΤΑΧΥΤΗΑΝ — Reduce speed
ΕΡΓΑΕΠΙΤΗΣΟΔΟΥ — Road works in Progress
ΑΝΩΜΑΑΙΑΟΔΟΣΤΡΩΜΑΤΟΣ — Bad road surface
ΑΠΑΓΟΡΕΥΕΤΑΙΤΟΠΡΟΣΠΕΡΑΣΜΑ — No overtaking
ΤΕΛΟΣ ΑΠΗΓΟΡΕΥΜΕΝΗΣ ΖΩΝΗΣ — End of no-overtaking
ΠΑΡΑΚΑΜΠΤΗΡΙΟΣ —Diversion
ΜΟΝΟΔΡΟΜΟΣ — One-way traffic

ΠΟΡΕΙΑ ΥΠΟΧΡΕΩΤΙΚΗ ΔΕΞΙΑ — Keep right
ΑΠΑΓΟΡΕΥΕΤΑΙΗΣΤΑΘΜΕΥΣΙΣ — No parking
ΑΔΙΕΞΟΔΟΣ — No through road

Accidents and Legal Advice

In the event of an accident involving personal injury or damage to property, both the law and your insurance require that it is reported to the police (☎ 0671 22200).

ELPA offer free legal advice concerning Greek legislation on car accidents and insurance.

Breakdowns

It is a legal requirement to place a warning triangle 100m/yds behind the car. Next step is to contact the car hire agency or if the car is private, contact Elpa by dialling 104. Elpa has reciprocal arrangements with European motoring organisations, like the British AA.

DISABLED FACILITIES

Whilst there is an awareness of this problem, few practical steps have been taken to improve matters. As yet only the international hotels provide anything like adequate facilities. Outside Argostoli, very few places have pavements and where present they are often full of trees

Preceding page: Old priest at Ag Gerassimos

making passage difficult in places. Ramps up and down pavements are few and far between.

ELECTRICITY

Mains electricity is supplied at 220 volts AC. Electrical equipment should be fitted with a continental two pin plug or an appropriate adapter used. A wide selection of adapters for local plugs to interchange between two and three pin (not UK three pin) are available cheaply on the island.

EMERGENCY TELEPHONE NUMBERS

Since Kefalonia is relatively new to tourism, emergency services are not yet organised. First point of contact is the tourist police, ☎ 0671 22200, who should be able to offer further guidance.

GREEK TIME

Greek normal time is 2 hours ahead of GMT. The clocks advance one hour for summertime starting the last Sunday in March and ending the last Sunday in September.

America and Canada: Greek normal time is ahead of time in America, 7 hours ahead of Eastern Standard, 8 hours ahead of Central, 9 hours ahead of mountain and 10 hours ahead of Pacific Time

Australia and New Zealand; Greek normal time is 7½ hours behind South Australia, 8 hours behind New South Wales, Tasmania and Victoria and 10 hours behind time in New Zealand. These differences relate to GMT but, to take into account clock changes for Daylight Saving hours, the following corrections should be made: add 1 hour to these differences from late September to the end of March and subtract 1 hour from late March to the end of September.

HEALTH CARE

For minor ailments like headaches, mosquito bites or tummy upsets, head for the chemist shop *(farmakion)*. If you need a further supply of prescription drugs make sure to take a copy of your prescription and the chances are that you will be able to get them, and cheaply too. Pharmacies are open normal shop hours and most seem to speak English. Certain chemist shops are on rota to provide a 24 hour service and information for the nearest is posted in the pharmacy window.

If it is a doctor or dentist you require, the chemist shop should again be able to assist. The island is not short of English-speaking doctors and dentists.

Problems really start if hospital treatment is required. European countries have reciprocal arrangements with the Greeks for free medical treatment, subject to certain restrictions. For this reason British visitors should take an E111 form obtained from the Post Office. The

Following page: A shrine at Ag Gerassimos

Above: Taking the ferry

Below: The theatre at Argostoli

story does not end there. To operate the scheme you need to find the local Greek Social Insurance office (IKA) who, after inspecting your E111, will direct you to a registered doctor or dentist. If you are in a region remote from the IKA office in Argostoli then you must pay privately for your treatment and present your bills to an IKA official before you leave the island. Up to half your costs may be refunded. The best answer is to ensure that you have adequate holiday insurance cover.

Emergency treatment, sunburn, broken bones etc, is free in state hospitals. The situation is less happy if you require treatment as an in-patient. In many of these hospitals, nursing care is restricted only to medical treatment and it is left to the family to supply general nursing care, drinks, food and even blankets.

It is generally preferable to activate private medical insurance.

HEALTH HAZARDS

Stomach upsets are perhaps the most common ailment. The excessive olive oil used in cooking and over salads can be a cause of queezy stomachs so take care with oily foods, at least to start with. The digestive system adjusts to this within a few days and you can soon eat giant beans swimming in oil without fear. Squeeze plenty of fresh lemon over your food to counter the oil and, if still troubled, an acidic drink, like Coca-Cola, helps to settle things. Drinking wine to excess can

cause similar symptoms too. More serious are the upsets caused by bad water and bad food. Generally on Kefalonia it is better to drink bottled water which is freely available and cheap in the shops and supermarkets. Avoiding food poisoning is not always possible but there are elementary precautions that can help. Many tavernas prepare cooked dishes for the lunch time trade and these are left keeping warm until finally sold. If they are still there in the evening, and they often are, avoid them. Ask for something which will require grilling or roasting.

See also Mosquitoes.

HOLIDAY INSURANCE

Whichever holiday insurance you choose, make sure that the cover for medical expenses is more than adequate. It helps too if there is an emergency 24 hour contact to take care of arrangements, including repatriation if necessary. Injuries caused whilst taking part in certain hazardous pursuits are normally excluded from medical cover. Look carefully at the specified hazardous pursuits; in recent times, injuries caused by riding a moped or motorbike have been added to the list by some insurers.

INTERNATIONAL DIALLING CODES

Codes from Greece are as follows: UK and Northern Ireland 0044: United States and Canada 001: Australia 0061: New Zealand: 0064. See also Telephone Services.

LANGUAGE

Many Greeks speak good English and they certainly do on Kefalonia. Children learn it in state schools and most of them attend private schools as well. After all, English is the official second language in Greece and all official notices are presented in Greek and English, at least the more recent notices. Therein lies the danger. It is all too easy to expect and rely on every Greek to speak English which is clearly not the case when you move into country areas.

Some knowledge of the Greek language is not only useful to help you get by, but can enhance enormously the pleasure of your holiday. The Greeks really warm to you if you make the slightest effort with their language. Do not worry about perfection in pronunciation in the beginning, just give it a go. The Greeks are very outgoing and, if they have any English, they will try it out no matter how fractured it is. Take a leaf from their book. As long as you make an effort, the Greeks will love you for it and once you can string a few words together you might find their hospitality overwhelming.

Perhaps the biggest hurdle to getting started is the Greek alphabet itself. If you take a little time to study it, you will find it is not really so different. Isolate the letters which are unique to the Greek alphabet and the remainder generally follow the sequence of the English alphabet. The language is phonetic so time taken over learning the sounds of the letters will be well rewarded in subsequent progress. Two pieces of advice to get you started on the right foot. (1) Treat all vowels equally and do not attempt to lengthen them. (2) Avoid breaking a word down into syllables as in English, instead, follow the stress pattern indicated by the accent in the word.

The Alphabet

Dipthongs
ai **e** in met
an **av** as in avoid or **af** in after
eu **ev** as in ever or **ef** as in left
oi **e** as in feet
ou **oo** as in mood

Double consonants
mp — **b** at the beginning of words; **mb** in the middle
vt — **d** at the beginning of words; **nd** in the middle
tz — **dz** as in adze
gg = **ng** — in the middle of a word
gk = **g** — g at the beginning; ng in the middle

Numbers

The numbers 1, 3 and 4 (and all numbers ending in them) have three forms, masculine, feminine and neteur. In this list the phonetic words are given in place of the Greek.

1 — ena (n), enas (m) or mia (f)
2 — theo
3 — tria (n), tris (m & f)

Following page: Svoronata

4 — tessera (n), tessaris (m & f)
5 — pende
6 — eksi
7 — efta
8 — octo
9 — enya
10 — theka
11 — entheka
12 — thotheka
13 — theka tria
14 — theka tessera
        etc up to twenty
20 — eekosee
21 — eekosee ena (n & m), mia (f)
30 — treeanda
40 — seranda
50 — peninda
60 — eksinda
70 — evthominda
80 — ogthonda
90 — eneninda
100 — ekato
130 — ekato treeanda
200 — thea-kosea
300 — tria-kosea
1000 — hilia

Days of the week:

Monday — Theftera
Tuesday — Treetee
Wednesday — Tetartee
Thursday — Pemptee
Friday — Paraskevee
Saturday — Savato
Sunday — Kiriakee

Months of the year:
January — Eeanuareos
February — Fevruareos
March — Marteos
April — Apreeleos

May — Maeos
June — Eeuneos
July — Eeuleos
August — Avyustos
September — Septemvreos
October — Octovreos
November — Noemvreos
December — Thekemvreos

Useful phrases

Yes — neh
No — ockee
Please — parakalo
Thank you — efharreesto
Hello and goodbye — yasas
Good morning — kaleemera
Good evening — kaleespera
Goodnight — kaleeneekta
How are you? — tee kanete?
Do you speak English? —
       meelatee angleeka
When? — poteh?
I want — thelo

Where is/are? — poo eene?
... the post office? — poo eene to takeethromeeo?
... the tourist office — poo eene to grafeeo toureesmoo?
... the museum? — poo eene to mooseeo?
... the bus station — poo eene o stathmos ton leoforeeon?
... the toilets — poo eene ee tooaletes?

Hotel — ksenothoheeo
Perhaps you have.. — meepos ekehteh
.. a single room — ena mono thomateeo

Preceding page: In the noonday sun

...a double room — ena theeplo thomateeo
...with bath — meh banyeeo
...with shower — meh dush

Shop — to magazee
Market — agora
How much? — posso?
How many? — possa?
How much does it cost? — posso kanee?
How much do they cost? — posso kanoonee?
Open/closed — anikto/kleesto
Stamp(s) — gramatossimo/gramatossima
Envelope(s) — fakelo(a)
One kilo — ena kilo
Half a kilo — meeso kilo
Two kilo — theo kila
Apple(s) — meelo(a)
Orange(s) — portokalee(eea)
Tomatoes — domates
Cucumber — angouree
Lettuce — maroolee

Doctor — yatros
Pharmacy — farmakeeo
Hospital — nosokomeeo
Police — asteenomeea

Place names

With no official transliteration, the latinisation of the Greek alphabet is open to various interpretations which leads to much confusion. Vowel sounds, especially **e** and **i**, do not always strictly correspond so there is a tendency to substitute the more phonetically correct. Some single consonants have no strict equivalent either, such as X, pronounced as the **ch** in loch, and this is Latinised to **ch**, which is a mile away phonetically, or **h** which is a little better. The village of Xora appears as Chora or Hora. All these difficulties are reflected in the spelling of place names. Pick up three different maps and it is more than likely that many of the same villages will have three different spellings. The philosophy adopted for this book is firstly to follow the spelling observed on the sign outside the village or, since many villages are without name boards, use the spelling which leads to a more accurate pronunciation.

LOST PROPERTY

This should be reported immediately to the Tourist Police, Port area, Argostoli ☎ 0671 22200. It is particularly important if an insurance claim is to be made.

MAPS

On the whole, maps of Kefalonia are more accurate than for many other Greek islands but still not wholly reliable. The main roads are accurately marked but the position of joining roads does not necessarily relate to reality nor does the indication of the surface. Generally, the signposting is fairly good on the island with the Greek signs displayed first and the Latinised version a little nearer the junction.

Following page: Argostoli fisherman

Mosquitoes

Mosquitoes feed most actively at dusk and dawn but they can still be a nuisance throughout the evening and the night. If you sit or dine outside in the evening, particularly near trees, either cover up your arms and legs or use insect repellent. For the hotel room, an electric machine which slowly vaporises a pellet is very effective, especially with the windows closed, and there are sprays available for more instant results if intruders are spotted. Anthisan anti histamine cream is an effective calming treatment for bites, particularly if applied immediately.

Museums

There is a charge for admission except on a Sunday when entrance is free to all but private museums. Monday is now the general closing day.

The museums are closed too, or open only for a short while, on certain public holidays which include 1 January, 25 March, Good Friday and Easter Monday, 1 May and 25 and 26 December. In addition they have half-days on Shrove Monday, Whitsunday, 15 August, 28 October and Epiphany, 6 January.

National Tourist Office

The Greek National Tourist Office in Argostoli is located in the Port area, ☎ 0671 22248.

Newspapers and Magazines

The Financial Times, most British newspapers, a selection from European countries and the Herald Tribune are usually available in virtually all centres of tourism. Mostly they are one day late and sometimes more. Expect a fair mark up in price. The place to look for newspapers is in the tourist shops, supermarkets and at the kiosks (*periptera*) where you will see them displayed on racks or along the counter.

A selection of English and European magazines is also available.

Nightlife

Kefalonia is not exactly renowned for its nightlife and the disco in Argostoli is only open at weekends. Things are slowly livening up in the resorts where the nightlife can be found in the bars and in some restaurants which organise Greek dancing.

Nudism

Topless bathing is commonplace on all public beaches on Kefalonia. Nude bathing is not acceptable on public beaches but is practised with discretion on some of the more remote and secluded beaches.

Pets

Cats and dogs require health and

Preceding page: End of the day!

rabies inoculation certificates issued by a veterinary authority in the country of origin not more than 12 months (cats 6 months) and not less than 6 days prior to arrival.

PHARMACIES

Pharmacies open Monday and Wednesday 8am–2.30pm. Tuesday, Thursday, and Friday 8am–2pm and 5–8pm and Saturday 8am–1pm. There is also a duty rosta for Pharmacies so that at least one in the vicinity is open on Saturday and Sunday. Usually a note on the door of the pharmacy details the duty chemist.

PHOTOGRAPHY

Signs which show a picture of a camera crossed out indicate a prohibited area for photography. Notices of this kind are posted near every military establishment, no matter how small or insignificant. Disregard this at your peril. The Greeks are still paranoiac about security and anyone found using a camera in a prohibited zone faces unpleasant consquences. The photographer is normally held in custody whilst the film is developed and inspected. It could mean overnight detention.

Photography with a camera mounted on a tripod is prohibited in museums as is the use of flash in some. Video cameras are often subject to a fee.

Outdoors, the light for photography is brilliant. Summer haze can cause difficulties with distant shots but the use of a UV or Skylight filter is helpful here. Some of the clearest days occur in spring when a dry east wind blows. Midday light is harsh and contrasty, mornings and evening provide the best lighting conditions for serious photography.

POSTAL SERVICES

Post Offices open on weekdays from 7.30am–2pm. They are closed on Saturday and Sunday.

Stamps (grammatosima) can be purchased at the post office, sometimes at a special counter, or at a kiosk (periptero). They are also available in many shops and some of the larger hotels but at a slightly increased price.

Letters from Greece to overseas destinations are delivered fairly speedily, 4/6 days for Europe, 6/8 for America and longer for Australia and New Zealand. For a speedier delivery, ask for express post on which there is a fairly modest surcharge but it cuts 2/3 days off the delivery time.

A telegram, telex or fax can be sent from the telephone office, the OTE although some tour agency offices also provide a service.

PUBLIC HOLIDAYS AND FESTIVALS

The Greek calendar overflows with red letter days; public holidays, Saints days and festivals. On public holidays, banks, shops and offices are closed although restaurants and tavernas normally stay open. Public transport is often interrupted too, reverting either to a Sunday service or to none at all. Petrol stations also close for many of the holidays. The days to watch out for are;

1 January — New Year's Day
6 January — Epiphany
25 March — Greek
        Independence Day;
Monday before Lent — Clean
        Monday
April — Good Friday & Easter
        Monday
1 May — May Day
21 May — Ionian Day,
        commemorating union
        with Greece
Whit Monday
15 August — Assumption of the
        Blessed Virgin Mary
28 October — 'Ochi' Day
25 December — Christmas Day
26 December — Boxing Day

Easter is variable and does not always coincide with Easter throughout the rest of Europe.

Name-days are one reason why the calendar is so full of celebrations. It has been a long tradition for Greeks to ignore birthdays to celebrate instead the special day of their saint, and there are a lot of saints. If you see people wandering around with cake boxes neatly tied with fancy ribbon, or bunches of flowers or unusual activity around one of the many churches, then the chances are that it is a name day. The custom is for the person celebrating to offer hospitality to friends, to neighbours and to almost anyone who will partake of a little ouzo and refreshments.

Some of the big name days to watch out for are:

23 April — St. George's day; all Georges everywhere celebrate their special day but in addition it is also the national day of Greece.
21 May — Saints Konstantinos and Eleni.
29 June — St. Peter and St Paul
15 August — Assumption of the Blessed Virgin Mary. The is the day when millions of Marias celebrate and an important day in the religious calendar often marked by local pilgrimages or festivals.
8 November — for all Michaels and Gabriels.
6 December — the feast of St. Nicholas.

Easter, the biggest and the most important celebration of the year and the arrival of Carnival time starts the long build up. This festival takes place throughout the three weeks before Lent and may commence as early as late January. Fancy dress is an important part of the tradition throughout the whole of Greece. It arises from the period of Turkish occupation when the Greeks were banned from conducting these celebrations. Driven under cover, festivities continued with people disguised to prevent recognition. Now it is firmly rooted into the custom and fancy dress and costumes are worn at all events. The children wander the streets in fancy dress and traditionally show defiance by wearing their disguises on the last school day of Carnival.

All this comes to an abrupt end with a complete change of mood on 'Clean Monday' (Kathari Deutera), the Monday before Lent. This is a public holiday when families traditionally exodus to the country to fly kites and to picnic, which mostly means heading to a taverna. Special meat-free menus are the order of the day.

It is back to the quiet life throughout Lent which is still strictly observed by many, especially in country regions. Serious preparations for Easter start on Maundy Thursday. How hens are persuaded to lay so actively for the occasion remains a mystery but shoppers are out buying eggs, not by the tens but by the hundreds. The rest of the day is spent in boiling the eggs and dying them red in the process. The colour red is supposed to have protective powers and the first egg dyed belongs to the Virgin.

Good Friday is a day of complete fast and widely observed. In tourist regions tavernas are open and life goes on as normal but in country areas it can be difficult or impossible to find food. Yellow or brown 'impure' candles are on sale everywhere ready for the evening church service. The sombre mood of the day is heightened by the continual tolling of church bells. It is a day for remembering their own dead; graves are visited and wreaths are laid. In the evening, the burial of Christ is the most moving and widely attended service in the whole of the Greek Orthodox calendar. The Epitaphios, the funeral bier of Christ, is centre stage in the services which start around 9pm. Garlanded with fresh flowers and with a gilded canopy, the Epitaphios bearing the coffin of Christ is ceremoniously taken from church in dig-nified candlelit procession followed by silent mourners and accompanied by bands playing solemn music. The processions from all the local churches meet in the town square for a further short service. This is the most poignant moment of the evening, cafes close, tavernas close and there is not one Greek who would willingly miss it. The processions return slowly to their churches, stopping at each street corner for a short prayer.

Saturday brings an air of expectancy. For the evening service, yellow candles are replaced with white. Funereal drapes are removed in the churches and decorations of laurel and myrtle take their place. In dimly lit churches everywhere, services begin. Slowly the light intensity increases reaching full brightness at midnight when priests triumphantly chant 'Christ is risen' *(Christos anesti)*. The sanctuary doors open to show that the Epitaphios is empty. Light from the priest's candle is passed to the congregation and that flame is rapidly passed from candle to candle until it reaches the waiting crowds outside. Fire crackers drown the clamour of the church bells as the crowd erupts in joyous celebration and greetings of *'Christos anesti'* ring out loudest of all. The crowds disperse shortly carefully protecting their burning candle; it is a good omen to enter the home with the flame still burning and make a sooty sign of the cross on the door lintel.

Sunday is a day of out and out rejoicing. The big occasion of the day is roasting the lamb or goat. Charcoal fires are lit early in the morning and the spit roasting is done with loving care over some 5 hours with copious quantities of ouzo or retsina to help things along. All those red eggs now appear and are used in friendly competition. Each contestant taps their egg hard enough to break an opponent's but not their own.

Easter Monday has no special ceremonies or rituals and passes as any normal public holiday.

Cultural Events

Religious fairs, *panayiria,* are commonplace in the summer months. *Panayiria* are a celebration of the name day of a particular church or monastery and usually held in the vicinity of the establishment. Celebrations are colourful, often beginning on the eve of the name day and continue throughout the actual day. Eating, drinking and dancing are central to any celebration for the Greeks so the barbecue is certain to be in operation. When the crowds are big enough, the vendors join in selling just about anything, baubles, bangles and beads.

Ag Gerassimos, the island's patron saint, is celebrated twice a year, on 16 August, the anniversary of his death, and on 20 October marking the day his body was lifted.

A word of warning too. Each town and village has its own saint's day and sometimes, depending on the local whim and the phase of the moon, a holiday is called. This decision is often not taken until the day before so there is no way you can plan for such eventualities.

PUBLIC TOILETS

The most usual sign is WC with figures to indicate ladies *(gynaikon)* and gents *(andron)*. Cafés provide the best hope of toilets even though it may be necessary to purchase a drink.

PUBLIC TRANSPORT

Buses

The bus service on Kefalonia is good and it offers a reliable way to see the island, The biggest problem is buses on popular routes get overcrowded in season and it may be difficult to board one at an intermediate stop.

Printed timetables are usually available from the Tourist Office. The frequency of services is much less in winter but builds up as the tourist season gets underway. Throughout May the timetable changes weekly until the service reaches its maximum frequency sometime in June which is then held until early September. The timetable holds equally from Monday through to Saturday but Sunday sees a reduction in the number of buses to about half.

Taxis

Taxis are freely available in Argostoli and most of the tourist resorts.

Greek taxi drivers are not the most honest in the world and it pays either to check the price before the journey, if it is for a lengthy ride, or better still, insist that the meter be used. This displays the cumulative fare in drachmas. The rate of charges and surcharges are all fixed. Legitimate small surcharges are allowed for a sizeable piece of luggage, for attending an airport or port for the benefit of passengers, and for late night or very early morning travel. Surcharges are permitted too at holiday times, especially Christmas and Easter. Picking up a second fare is allowed too so you may find yourself sharing a taxi.

SHOPPING

Regulations on opening hours have changed recently to adjust to market needs. Different regions have their own views on this so there is now greater confusion than ever over opening times. Big supermarkets and department stores open: Monday to Friday 8am to 8pm. Saturday 8am to 3pm. Other shops open Monday and Wednesday 8am to 2.30pm. Tuesday, Thursday, and Friday 8am to 2pm and 5 to 8pm and Saturday 8am to 1pm.

In tourist areas, shopping hours are much more relaxed. Tourist shops and supermarkets in particular are open all day long but butchers, bakers and the like tend to observe more restricted hours.

SPORTS AND PASTIMES

Windsurfing :
Many of the small bays and coves are ideally suited to this sport and boards can be hired in most holiday resorts. Lessons for beginners are generally available too at rates which are still very reasonable.

Water-skiing and Jet skiing:
Available at some of the larger resorts as well as parascending.

Scuba diving:
Strictly prohibited unless in the control of a recognised diving school and only in designated areas. With so many antiquities in the waters around Greece, it is forbidden to remove anything from the sea bed and infringements normally result in a prison sentence.

Tennis:
Courts are mostly to be found in the better class hotels but some allow non residents to use the facilities for a charge.

Horse riding:
There are opportunities for horse riding, by Lourdas Beach hotel for

Clothes Sizes

Mens Suits:

UK/US	36	38	40	42	44	46	48
Greece	46	48	50	52	54	56	58

Dress Sizes:

UK	8	10	12	14	16	18
US	6	8	10	12	14	16
Greece	34	36	38	40	42	44

Below: Kalamia beach

Above: Poros beach

example, but otherwise it will be necessary to enquire locally.

Walking:

There are opportunities for walking but the only organised information is that provided in a leaflet issued by the tourist office in Argostoli. There is also a leaflet for walking on Ithaka.

Sailing:

This is extremely popular in this area and most resorts have boats for hire. Yachts are available for hire in Fiskardo either with or without crews if the charterer can prove competence with a recognised proficiency certificate.

SUNBATHING

Sunburn and sunstroke can easily spoil your holiday and considerable care needs to be exercised, especially in the early days. The sun is very burning even on a hazy day so great care is needed in protecting yourself and high factor sun creams should be used. Crawling beneath a parasol is not necessarily the full answer since the sun's rays reflect to some extent from the sand. Avoid, if possible, sunbathing in the middle of the day, from 10am until around 2pm when the sun is at its highest and most direct. Sun creams help considerably but, at least for the first few days, take some very light clothing to cover up and control the exposure of your skin to the sun. A slowly acquired tan lasts longer.

Even mild sunburn can be painful and may cause a chill feeling but if fever, vomiting or blistering occur then professional help is essential.

SWIMMING

There is good swimming off many beaches on the island but there is no system of warning flags to indicate unsafe conditions. It is absolutely essential to use common sense when the sea is rough or strong currents are flowing and avoid taking unnecessary risks at all times.

TELEPHONE SERVICES

Hotels usually offer a telephone service, often from the room, but expect to pay a premium for the convenience.

Telephone booths on the island have now been modernised to take phonecards and these are both convenient and economical. Cards, loaded with 100 units, are available often from the shop or *periptero* nearest the booth and the cost per unit is exactly the same as the OTE (Telecommunications office) charge. There is an OTE office in Argostoli Town where metered phones are available with a pay at the desk system. The advantage of the OTE is that payment is made only for the units used whereas a card may be more units than required.

In the main holiday resorts a number of tourist agencies offer a telephone service and often call themselves telephone exchanges. Although sometimes convenient, they are run for profit so expect to pay a higher rate.

International dialling codes from Greece are as follows: UK and Northern Ireland 0044: United States and Canada 001: Australia 0061: New Zealand: 0064.

TIPPING

There are no hard and fast rules on tipping, especially since bills by law already include a 17 per cent service. Normally, the Greeks simply leave behind the small change after a meal and perhaps the best guide is to reward only for good service in a restaurant. Taxi drivers expect a tip as does the chamber maid in the hotel otherwise it is entirely by discretion.

WATER

Sources of drinking water vary on the island and all should be regarded as not suitable to drink unless otherwise advised. Bottled water is freely available.

INDEX

A

Ag Efimia   84
Ag Gerassimos   85
Agrapidiaes Pass   77, 84
Angonas   73
Anti Samos   45, 80
Argostoli   16, 45
   Ag Nikolaos   52
   Ag Theodori Lighthouse   53
   Archaeological Museum   49
   Church of Ag Spiridon   52
   Drapano Bridge   52
   Greek Orthodox
      Cathedral   52
   Katavothres   53
   Kefalos Theatre   49
   Korgialenios Cultural and
      Historical Museum   49
   Korgialenios Library   52
   Lithostroto   52
Arts and Culture   29
Assos   17, 73
Athens   97
   Acropolis   100
   Agora   100
   Dexameni Square   105
   Flea Market   108
   Hill of the Muses
      (Filopappou Hill)   104
   Kolonaki Square   105
   Plaka   108
   The National Archaeological
      Museum   105
   Tower of the Winds   108
Avithos Beach   88

C

Climate   13

D

Drogarati Cave   77

E

Emblisi Beach   76

F

Fiskardo   17, 53, 76
Flora and Fauna   29
Food and Drink   20

G

Geography   9
Geology   9
Gradakia beach   44

H

History   32

I

Ithaka   61
   Anogi 69
   Cave of the Nymphs   65

Dexia   65
Frikes   72
Perahori   68
Pisso Aetos   65
Platrithias   72
Pollis 69
Stavros 69
Vathy   65

K

Kalamia beach   44
Karavomylos   81
Kato Katelios   16, 92

L

Lassi   16, 44
Lepeda   61
Lepeda beach   45
Lixouri   17, 57
   Church of Ag
      Haralambos   60
   Library and Museum   60
Lourdas Beach   16, 44, 92

M

Makrys Gialos   44
Markopoulo   89
Mazarakata   88
Melissani Cave   81
Mount Ainos 44

Mount Atros   92
Myrtos Beach   45, 73

O

Olympia   93
   Archaeological Museum   97
   Nymphaion Fountain   97
   The Palaistra   96
   The Stadium   97
   The Temple of Hera   96
   The Temple of Zeus   97
   Treasuries   97

P

Platys Gialos   44
Poros   16, 45, 89

R

Robola Producer's
      Co-operative   85

S

Sami   16, 80
Skala   16, 44, 92
St George's Castle   88
Svoronata   16

T

The People   25
Tzanata   89